Sartre and No Child Left Behind

Sartre and No Child Left Behind

An Existential Psychoanalytic Anthropology of Urban Schooling

Darian M. Parker

LEXINGTON BOOKS
Lanham • Boulder • New York • London

Published by Lexington Books
An imprint of The Rowman & Littlefield Publishing Group, Inc.
4501 Forbes Boulevard, Suite 200, Lanham, Maryland 20706
www.rowman.com

Unit A, Whitacre Mews, 26-34 Stannary Street, London SE11 4AB

British Library Cataloguing in Publication Information Available

Library of Congress Cataloging-in-Publication Data

Parker, Darian M., 1978-
   Sartre and no child left behind : an existential psychoanalytic anthropology of urban schooling /
Darian M. Parker.
      pages cm
   Includes bibliographical references and index.
   ISBN 978-0-7391-9159-0 (cloth : alk. paper) -- ISBN 978-0-7391-9160-6 (electronic)
1. Education, Urban--Social aspects--United States. 2. Education, Urban--Psychological aspects--
United States. 3. United States. No Child Left Behind Act of 2001. 4. Psychoanalysis and anthropolo-
gy. 5. Existential psychology. 6. Sartre, Jean-Paul, 1905-1980. I. Title.
   LC5131.P35 2015
   370.9173'2--dc23
                              2015021005

Printed in the United States of America

This book is dedicated to my mother, Florine Edith Parker, without whom none of this would have been possible, and to my grandmother, Mozelle Morrison, who foretold of this moment thirty-five years ago.
I love you both dearly.

Contents

Preface

In the fall of 2006, I answered a Craigslist advertisement posted by an independent tutoring agency. The company was conducting a search for tutors to work with seventh and eighth graders at Promise Academy, a charter school that is part of a broader educational and social work agency in New York City known as the Harlem Children's Zone (HCZ). Promise Academy had contracted Wyzant to help the former's students raise their scores on the end-of-year state-administered examinations in math and English Language Arts (ELA).

These scores were absolutely essential to the life of Promise Academy and to the Harlem Children's Zone, a multi-million-dollar non-profit corporation. In addressing the social and economic needs of the Harlem community—which historically has had some of the highest rates of crime, health maladies, and educational challenges in the nation—the Harlem Children's Zone is endeavoring to accomplish a very formidable goal: to "end the cycle of generational poverty" in Harlem (www.hcz.org). In order to accomplish this feat, HCZ has to continue to demonstrate to its many funders and supporters that its innovative methods of youth and community development are yielding remarkable results, chief of which are increases in standardized test scores. Both HCZ and its impressive constituency of funders did not develop their passion for math and ELA test scores in a vacuum, however. They are mirrors of the New York City Public School System—which privileges these tests as markers of students' and schools' merits—and national educational policies, which have made these particular tests the chief criteria for schools to receive federal funding (McGuinn, 2006).

I interviewed for, acquired, and eagerly accepted the position on December 4, 2006. This date also marked the beginning of my three-year immersion into the total field of the New York City Public School District. The tutoring format was of a nature to which I had not been previously accustomed. During the final period of the school day, proceeding into after-school hours—from 3 p.m. to 7 p.m.—select students were obligated to receive "pull-outs." In order to receive a pull-out, students had to meet one or more of the following criteria (not that these students necessarily counted these sessions as a privilege): one had to have received a failing grade (1 or 2 on a 5-point scale) on either the math or ELA state exam the previous year, a D or an F in one or more of his or her core math and ELA classes, or the after-school program coordinators would require a student to attend a session if the former felt that a child needed to be productively occupied on a given day. The previous year's state test scores were the primary determinants, however. If a student had failed one exam, then that individual received two pull-outs per week. If the student had failed both the math and the ELA exams, then he or she merited four weekly pull-outs.

The tutoring sessions received their name because students were literally "pulled out" of either their final class period (if the session occurred from 3 p.m. to 4 p.m.), or one of their most cherished after-school activities. For the majority of the students enrolled in Promise Academy, pull-outs accounted for about one-half to two-thirds of their after-school time every week.

I got to know and love all of the students to whom I had been personally assigned, as well as those who were in the charges of other tutors. Most of us tutors cared about these children and believed whole-heartedly in HCZ's mission. However, our commitment to the organization could not stem the inevitable tide of resistance that came from the students. Over weeks, months and for some, successive years of regular pull-outs, the students became increasingly hostile to the idea of one-on-one tutoring sessions and to those who administered these sessions: the tutors. The students felt that they were being tormented and unfairly punished. They rebelled in ways large and small. When a tutor would come to the classroom to retrieve his or her student, the former was subject to encounter a boisterously plaintive, "I don't want to go!" or "I hate pull-outs!" A tutor might arrive to discover that a student had hidden in the closet, underneath a desk, or had already been excused for what turned into an inordinately long departure to the bathroom. Sometimes students would go willingly, yet cleverly, with tutors, then make a quick dash to another area of the building. It got to the point in which these varied acts of rebellion became commonplace.

Nevertheless, the rebels could rarely escape their fates. Through threats of calling home, revoking recreational privileges, and the like, students would finally be persuaded into participating. They would go with their tutors reluctantly, half-withdrawn. And all of us tutors and students would fight our way through the sessions. Exhausted, we might somehow find the fortitude and imagination we needed to be productive, stimulating, and stimulated. Most of the time, we all managed to leave with the one reward that was daily being called into question, and threatening to unravel due to its inherent and socially conditioned volatility: a mutual like for the other person.

During my years tutoring at Promise Academy, the school saw the remarkable results that HCZ needed to appease its funders. The students' math and ELA scores exceeded (and continue to exceed) those of even wealthy school districts in New York City. Yet, despite HCZ's triumphs, I could not help but feel that the New York City Department of Education was ignoring other "results." Either these results had been classified as unimportant, been consigned to an inferior position within a more comprehensive hierarchy of results, or simply been rendered insignificant because they had been made to inhabit the realm of "process," which is altogether outside the hierarchy of results. For some scholars of education, particularly those concerned with the massive New York City Department of Education system, the unsung results concern the overall quality of education for the students. Diane Ravitch (2010), Thomas Poetter (2006), and Catherine Haerr (2005), for example, all lament the ways that the nation's emphasis on standardized testing, a hallmark of the 2001 No Child Left Behind (NCLB) legislation, has completely negated children's—particularly ethnic minority children in impoverished school districts—civic entitlement to a quality education. These scholars have also established causal links between the high-stakes testing milieu and the inability of ethnic minority students to successfully access the rights and privileges of the larger democratic society. Indeed, many scholars have sought to identify the social and academic sources of failure, hoping to find practical solutions to fix what many agree is a broken system (Chapman 2005, Choi and Piro 2009, DiPardo and Schnak 2004; Beveridge 2010; Eisner 2002; Garoian 2001; Bitz 2004; Winerip 2003; Kleinfield 2002; Lipman 2004; McNeil 2000; Capello 2004; Lewin and Medina 2003; Watanabe 2007; Wei 2002; Winter 2004; Wright 2008; Youdell and Gillborn 2000; Youdell 2004). Others, such as Maxine Greene (2007), Nel Noddings (2007), and Bruce Wilson (2001), are concerned that the inner, emotional lives of children become impoverished when the primary goal of educative rituals becomes the pursuit of satisfactory test scores.

The "result" that I wanted to understand was something more elusive than educational quality, which can be accessed through a study of curriculum standards and implementation. My object of interest was even more elusive than the students' emotional realities, which can be quite easily accessed through interviewing. I wanted to know who these children at Promise Academy were *becoming* in this particular academic environment. What were they implicitly and explicitly learning to value? How were their views of the world, themselves, and the experience of learning being molded? How were they being conditioned to inhabit the realities that were being co-constructed between themselves and the concentric levels of institutionality in which they were embedded?

Ultimately, I abandoned my urge to conduct an ethnographic study of Promise Academy; for, I became convinced that these students were "becoming" healthier, happier, more fulfilled, and principled human beings. There was copious unquantified and unquantifiable data to confirm this point. I witnessed their conversations, mannerisms, choices of clothes, and their ambitions be completely transformed over the course of the three years that I worked with them. I saw some go from being gang members to articulate, college-bound scholars. Some who bore the mark of intense trauma—having witnessed parents murdered right before their very eyes or having been the victims of sexual abuse—ceased to act out these traumas in reckless, self-destructive ways; some became fully functional, charismatic leaders in their school. *Results* such as these confirm the truth of the pronouncement that Geoffrey Canada has made frequently in his many public talks: that the Harlem Children's Zone is essentially "rescuing" the children in the Harlem community and altering the trajectory of their lives. Statistics further support Canada's claim. Over 90 percent of the organization's 2012 graduates, the very students that I had worked with for three years, are currently attending institutions of higher education.

From what, however, are the students of Promise Academy Charter School being rescued? What about those *public school* attendees who do not have the privilege of being "caught up in the rapture"? What of the schools that *these* students attend—un-enmeshed in a network of private funders, community supporters, tutoring contracts, and sophisticated social work interventions? Who were these students becoming? In an educative regime that is notorious for "teaching to the test," ignoring imperatives for a robust, holistic education, and the cultivation of character and civic principles, who would these students come to be?

The following chapters are my attempt to understand the "becoming" of urban poor children in the New York City Public School District. Attending this primary concern is a pressing methodological question: How does the anthropologist study this "becoming"? A series of corollary questions follow: What are the tools the researcher uses to access these complex fields of becoming? What critical lens is most effective for understanding the ethnographic data that are collected?

One of the most apparent solutions to my methodological queries was that I would simply need to employ very conventional models of ethnographic research. In order to understand the complex processes of becoming involved in these educative rituals, I knew that I must, to the extent possible, inhabit the very realities that the children lived within each day. I was to follow their same routes to school, sit in their classrooms, take part in their pedagogical rituals, and get to know the teachers and staff members who populated the school building.

After encountering many predictable barriers to the type of immersion that I needed for my research, I finally, through the kindness of one influential public school teacher (who would eventually become my primary informant), received an opportunity to study The Academy, which was in many ways representative of the plight faced by urban poor children in New York City public schools and in urban school districts across the country: it shared a building with three other schools; it was scheduled to close in two years (and after the study, it did indeed close) due to low academic performance, a high preponderance of in-school violence, and failing test scores; and it housed a student population that was predominately poor, African American, and Latina(o). The Academy was the prototypical "Title I School," or an institution recognized by the No Child Left Behind Act (NCLB) as having an exceedingly high proportion of academically and socially "disadvantaged" youth.

Many education scholars have deployed ethnographic methods to study the de facto effects of NCLB legislation upon school children in inner cities. The vast majority of these studies are meant to identify and explicate a fundamental irony of the legislation: while the act's express aim is to improve the quality of education for disadvantaged students, NCLB actually compromises the educational outcomes for this population (McGee 2006; Thompson-Shriver 2009; Booher-Jennings 2006; Berliner and Nichols 2005; Amrein and Berliner 2002; Gunzenhauser 2002, 2006; Hursh 2005; Pinzur 2003). In consulting this literature, however, I became aware that there is a dearth of models for conducting an ethnographic study that makes a robust attempt to understand the existential and affective consequences of this legislation upon the children themselves. There are scholars of American educational institutions, however, who do critique the current education scholarship's tendency to ignore the more "human" consequences of NCLB (Watanabe 2007; DiPardo 2004; Wei 2002; Greene 2007; Noddings 2007; Parlmer 2007; Southgate 2003; Barrier-Ferreira 2008). These scholars urge their peers to consider the emotional impact of NCLB upon teachers and students. Yet, none of these studies employ ethnographic methods. As a result, students' and teachers' own descriptions of their experiences, and even third-party descriptions of educational settings, are conspicuously absent.

The present study is a decided attempt to fill this void. My aim is twofold: to mine the complex processes by which children, faculty, and the institution of The Academy itself come to be; and preliminarily glean the very texture of how students and teachers actually experience The Academy. Ultimately, what follows is meant to be representative of the modes of becoming and experience that persist in urban poor school districts throughout New York City and the United States.

Acknowledgments

I must first thank my mother, Florine E. Parker, for being the guiding light in everything that I have ever done in life. All my critical, moral, and ethical sensibilities I have adopted from her and have seen their development by her sacrifices, seen and unseen. Thank you for your love, your selflessness, and all of your sacrifices. I would not have been able to do any of this without you. I love you dearly. Secondly, I must thank my grandmother, Mrs. Mozelle Morrison, who, when I was a child, foretold of this very moment. She, like my mother, has made innumerable sacrifices on my and my mother's behalf. I love you, grandma.

I would like to offer my sincerest gratitude to David Sequeira, Kelly Blackburn, Amy King, Francinia Williams, all anonymous reviewers, and the entire staff at Rowman & Littlefield and Lexington Books for your nurturing guidance throughout the completion of this project. Collectively and individually, you represent the highest ideals of the publishing process.

I offer a special thanks to Professor Kamari Clarke, who had been my advisor since I entered the Department of Anthropology at Yale. Your nurturing ways, efficiency, insight, theoretical rigor, and willingness to assist me at every turn of this process have been indispensable to this project and to my entire graduate career. Both my mother and I sincerely appreciate who you are and how you have enabled my development. To Professor Jafari Allen, I am ever indebted to you for your diligence throughout the revision process and your insistence that I channel my highest potential. Thank you for prompting me to go deeper in my consideration of African diasporic anthropological, philosophical, and psychoanalytic traditions. This work and my career prospects are a great deal better because of your sincerity, concern, and professional mentorship. Professor Tyson Lewis, your insights concerning the phenomenological tradition and educational philosophy have been absolutely invaluable to the development of this work. I sincerely thank you for your intellectual and personal generosity throughout this process, and your willingness to assist me each time that I reached out to you. I remain awed and edified by your seamless integration of complex philosophical and theoretical traditions.

It is often said that institutions are faceless and the antithesis of all that is human. Yet, I would be remiss if I did not acknowledge the Department of African American Studies, the Department of Anthropology, and Yale University for the defining role that they individually and collectively played in the completion of my graduate career and this work. I offer my sincerest thanks to each one of you.

To my primary informant, "Mr. Wheeler," thank you so much for granting me access to your school and to your world. I would not have been able to complete this project without you. You are truly a "paragon of virtue" and I love you dearly. I offer sincere thanks also to the executive director of the organization that connected me with Mr. Wheeler. In many ways, you are the reason that I was able to complete this project. I wish you nothing but success in your business and in life. Be blessed.

I have deep gratitude also for many special people in the departments of African American Studies and Anthropology at Yale. Mrs. Geneva Melvin, thank you so much for everything that you have done. You were truly my angel from the moment I entered Yale through to the very end. I love you and will never forget all that you have done for my mother and me. Janet Giarratano, I love you dearly. Thank you for being so quick, efficient, caring, and just. I'll always remember your contribution to my career at Yale. Karen Phillips, I am grateful to you for being so informative and helpful in so many ways. Thank you for being kind and efficient. I would also like to thank the following professors for guiding me through this experience in countless and invaluable ways: Elizabeth Alexander, Gerald Jaynes, Paul Gilroy, Hazel Carby, Harold Scheffler, William Kelly, Anne Underhill, Glenda Gilmore, Robert Farris Thompson, John Szwed, and Birgit Brander-Rasmussen.

I offer a sincere, heart-felt thank you to my dear friends, family, and extended family who have supported me while I embarked on this project: the Morrison/Parker family and my entire extended family in Winston-Salem, NC; the Miller family; Dionne Aminata Samb and the entire Thomas family, I love you all; Korri "Polo" Smith, I love you dearly; Terelle Jerricks and the Jerricks family; Stephanie Armstrong and the Armstrong family; Katynja McCory; Nzingha Camara and my entire Los Angeles dance family; Professor Calvin Warren; Professor Brandi Hughes; Dennis Bailey; Daaimah-Taalib-Din; Denica Abdur-Razzaaq; Thenayiz Jenkins; Isreal Heath; Aly Tatchol Camara and family; Dean George and the Afro-American Cultural Center at Yale; Mouminatou Camara and Sewee African Dance Company; Sandella Malloy, Frank Malloy, and Harambee Dance

Company; Abdel Salaam, Dyane Harvey, Dele Husbands, and Forces of Nature Dance Company; Mickey Davidson and Okra Dance Company; Maija Garcia and Organic Magnetics; Geoffrey Canada and Harlem Children's Zone, Inc.; David Gordon and Jen Gordon of Pinnacle Prep.

Lastly, I would like to thank my research subjects at both fieldsites. I especially thank the children of "The Academy," who shared their lives with me for nine months. I pray that your lives will be filled with love, happiness, and the profoundest sense of humanity. I love you all.

Introduction

Book Plan and Argument

The nature of my queries has prompted me to synthesize intellectual traditions that have, historically, been judged as incommensurable. My governing theoretical orientation is existentialist. A signifier that is at once empty and capacious depending on how one approaches its study, existentialism, for our purposes, is broadly defined as a manner of inquiry that specifically addresses questions of existence, being, and becoming. Pursuing existentialist theoretical aims, the study also necessarily deals with phenomenology, or the study of the texture and structures of consciousness and experience. The study takes its methodological inspiration from the existentialist and phenomenological philosophy of Sartre. Why evoke Sartre? Well, underneath his vast corpus of early work (and even some of his later work), is the premise that human beings are damned to remain conscious and involved, no matter the nature of the circumstance. We inevitably must confront our situations and rationalize them, even if these confrontations and rationalizations resolve themselves in various forms of dissociation and disavowal. It is this insistence upon the inevitable volition of consciousness that caused Sartre to reject the deterministic leanings of Freudian metatheory.

For Sartre, who we are is the result of a "fundamental project" of our own choosing, an idea to which he devotes an entire chapter in *Being and Nothingness*. He calls for an "existential psychoanalysis," the aim of which would be to unearth an individual's fundamental project as a way of explaining the course of that one's life, and, if the situation requires, to provide relief for various states of psycho-emotional dis-ease. In his memoirs and psycho-biographies, Sartre applies his existential psychoanalytic hypotheses to the study of various individual and collective predicaments. My analyses of

these works reveal that for a given individual a fundamental project is selected from a field of possibilities available to one in a given socio-historical
predicament. In other words, one's choice of being is inevitably constrained
by the situation into which he or she is propelled. What is more, I discovered
in Sartre's work that the phenomenological substance of experience, forged
at the nexus of consciousness and circumstance, manifests itself as particular
tropes. More than simply descriptors or indices of some more visceral state
of being, these tropes are themselves dense particles of experience, its ontological substance. I have termed these entities "tropological densities."

Founded upon Sartre's idea of fundamental projection, chapter 1 advances the notion of an existential psychoanalytic anthropology as a subfield
of the anthropology of consciousness. The chapter has six main subdivisions.
The first clears a path for the possibility of a legitimate science of consciousness by locating the disavowal of consciousness in the related discourses of
mathematical and analytical philosophy. In this section, I primarily engage
the work of Bertrand Russell to show that these branches of philosophy are
founded upon what is called "intuition," which references the cognitive activities of consciousness. With intuition constituting their origin and fundamental integrity, both mathematical and analytical philosophy proceed to
develop elaborate systems. Russell posits that these systems adhere to the
virtue of scientific "rigor." I argue that, in a clever but disingenuous rhetorical strategy, systematicity or what Russell calls "rigor," comes to displace
"intuition" as the defining feature of positivist inquiry. I further contend that
it has been this displacement that has posed a considerable challenge for the
category of "consciousness" itself as a credible entity—both as a purveyor of
valid scientific observations and as a legitimate object of investigation. I
propose that any science of consciousness, then, must reclaim intuition as the
displaced and disavowed predecessor to rigor. In short, I propose rigorous
intuition as the cardinal principle of a science of consciousness.

In the second section, I continue the proverbial path clearing by discuss-
ing some impediments to one particular science of consciousness: a distinctly
anthropological theory of consciousness. I propose that there are three main
challenges to this aim. First, there is the reign of a Boasian cultural particularism, meaning that anthropologists are reluctant to make claims that would
be universally applicable to all people and all human societies. I locate the
source of this reluctance in anthropology's skepticism about positivist science and the disciplinary guilt over anthropology's past complicity with the
colonialist project. The second impediment is the nebulous quality of consciousness itself. Consciousness is a composite entity that includes cognition,
emotion, and various modes of perceptual sensation. I argue that an important step toward having an anthropology of consciousness is to operationalize
the term itself. The third impediment regards issues of disciplinary ownership. Historically, consciousness has not been considered to *belong* to anthro-

pology; culture has. Cognition and emotion have belonged to psychology and medical science, and perception has been the property of medical science. Anthropology has owned culture, which presents a similar problem to that of consciousness: it is a composite entity. Culture includes various modalities of consciousness (belief, thought, etc.), social arrangements (which belong to the sociologist), ritual, and any other of the manifold constituents of what we acknowledge as context. Thus, in order to have an anthropological theory of consciousness, we must foreground consciousness in the grand collectivity of culture, and then proceed to operationalize consciousness. In the present work, I focus on cognition and affect, leaving aside perception for those experts in neurophysiology. I argue that in anthropology's global laboratory of sorts, the discipline has generated an impressive store of theoretical insights regarding cognition and affect—insights capable of standing on the world stage of interdisciplinary theory.

The third section synthesizes anthropological insights regarding cognition and emotion. I am specifically searching for what anthropologists have either implied or explicitly stated are the "mechanisms" of cognition and emotion. The discussion of cognition draws primarily from the anthropological literature on symbolic anthropology, cognitive anthropology, the anthropology of religion, and the anthropology of ritual. Here I define four mechanisms of cognition: (1) *symbolization*, (2) *systemization*, (3) *unconscious semiosis*, and (4) *resonation*. The first of these acknowledges that cognition involves the accretion of meanings. The second regards the fact that these accretions of meaning arrange themselves into systems of varying complexity. Unconscious semiosis indicates that accretions of meaning and systems of accretion reside in the terrain of pre-objective (unconscious) and objective (conscious) conceptualization, with infinite gradations in between. Finally, resonation references the power of symbolic configurations to effect transformations in the psychical, emotional, physiological, and cultural universes of humans— in other words, the capacity of symbols to powerfully resonate throughout our entire beings.

Section four deals with two defining attributes of affect: (1) *epiphenomenality* and (2) *comportmentality*. Epiphenomenality references the fact that emotions appear to be the epiphenomenal residue of particular existential conditions, while comportmentality regards emotion as a manner of comporting oneself to a particular cultural context. Section four continues the search for mechanisms of cognition and emotion by asking: What are the mechanisms by which meanings accrete to form symbols? What are the mechanisms by which the individual internalizes symbolic fields? What is the procedure by which symbolic networks activate the semi-autonomous register known as the pre-objective? How do people cultivate specific emotional repertoires, particularly those that are enduring? Where is the nexus between cognition and emotion? In order to answer these questions, I turn to Sartre and the Africana existentialist tradition.

The explication of Sartre's ideas concerning being, good faith, bad faith, and existential psychoanalysis, and a subsequent introductory analysis of my neologism "tropological densities" all comprise the content of section five. The chapter proceeds with an analysis of how the Africana existentialist tradition helps to extend Sartre's insights in ways amenable to an existential psychoanalytic anthropological praxis in general and to a study of African American subjects in particular. Heeding the admonition of Hortense Spillers, who famously proclaimed that any psychoanalysis of the African American condition must be founded upon the unique socio-historical con-figurations of African American people (1996), the chapter continues by considering how the racist symbolic order—instituted through the colonial encounter—constitutes the matrix within which the being of the Africana subject is forged. Spillers's admonition is the point of departure for my analysis of the works of various Africana existentialists. Chief among these, Lewis Gordon—who coined the term "Africana existentialism" and who also finds in Sartre an opportunity for theoretical interventions into the Africana life-world—insists that no consideration of Africana being can occur without understanding how blackness and whiteness are constituted as a semiological dyad. A common theme in the works of Africana existentialists, the dyadic nature of the symbolic order leads me to extend Sartre's insights, becoming attuned to the ways that fundamental projects are not only the productions of a solipsistic consciousness, but are constituted intersubjectively. Further-more, both Gordon and Cornel West argue that for Africana peoples, the racist symbolic order has the effect of limiting one's existential possibilities, a situation that Gordon calls "oppression." In other words, the field of pos-sible beings for the Africana subject is limited due to the proscriptive nature of the symbolic order.

The final section, section five, summarizes the insights of the foregoing sections to advance an existential psychoanalytic anthropology, which: (1) takes seriously the possibility of a rigorous intuition, (2) is nomothetic, yet grounded in cultural and historical particularity, (3) takes as foundational anthropological insights into the mechanisms of cognition and emotion, (4) is informed by Sartre's existential psychoanalysis and Africana existentialism.

Chapter 2 serves two functions: (1) it offers a brief historical overview of the No Child Left Behind legislation, and in doing so, (2) provides a context for the historically-constituted tropes that inform that legislation and the symbolic field of The Academy's students. I situate the law within the racial history of the United States, with particular focus on a series of legislative interventions that began in the nineteenth century with *Plessy v. Ferguson*. Next, I consider how the emphasis on high-stakes accountability testing is the direct outcome of twentieth-century electoral politics and international competition. The argument in this chapter is that the law and its implementation as high-stakes accountability standards have never been in the best interests of the children that they purportedly intend to help. Pedagogical subjects in disadvantaged communities were essentially "invisible" in the crafting of NCLB. The existential reverberations of this invisibility, therefore, serve to dehumanize the very people who must live within these sinister juridical prescriptions. The cumulative effect is that millions of schoolchildren return to the very predicament in which African Americans existed before the passing of *Brown v. Board of Education.*

Chapters 3 through 8 comprise the ethnographic bulk of the work. My argument concerning my field observations is as follows: The students and faculty members in The Academy "chose" who they would be as the result of intersubjective exchanges and within a social and symbolic order that was fundamentally racist and oppressive. The first five of these chapters investigate the complex webs of intersubjective experience and being-formation within The Academy. The portrait that emerges is of a school in which racist assumptions serve to negate the very worth of its predominantly black and Latina(o) student population. As a result, the building is ominous and inhospitable, and teachers degrade and refuse to teach students, the cumulative effect of which is that each day is a veritable pandemonium. In such an environment, the being-possibilities for a child are equally as limited and abject. Thus, what I saw overwhelmingly was students who wanted desperately to succeed, but did not have access to the resources to do so. Inevitably, many of the students chose to live in utopic discontent, and in earnest criticism of their predicament. Some chose to align themselves with the very substance of the racist architecture, becoming the very tropological densities of racial and cultural inferiority that accounted for the institutional structure of The Academy in the first place. All, however, were fundamentally powerless to alter the material and existential coordinates of their collective situation.

The beginning of this ethnographic sextuplet, chapter 3, explores how students and faculty existed within the forbidding physical space of the building itself. Chapter 4 considers the tropological densities of the "bad school" and "bad students" and how these densities served as mediums through which experiences and subjectivities were chosen. What I identified in the ethnographic record as the "androidal" quality of many of the teachers at The Academy comprises the substance of chapter 5. Here, I explore how the teachers came to "choose" to be androids, the effects of this choice upon students, and how students' choices regarding these androids continued to inform teachers' choices of being. The sixth chapter is an ethnographic analysis of the administration of the State English Language Arts Examination. Because the students at The Academy up to that point had been subjected to inferior teaching, many of them could only inhabit the testing period as beings that chose to dissociate, or subject themselves to the inevitable outcome of failure. Mr. Wheeler, who constituted a foil to the general malaise of The Academy, is the primary subject of chapter 7, which concentrates on how he was able to effectively destabilize the inertia of the tropological density of the bad school, the racist symbolic order, and assumptions about the inherent inferiority of ethnic minority students.

Chapter 8, the final ethnographic chapter, is an inquiry into the Department of Education's (DOE's) efforts to close Community Elementary School, also a Title I institution in New York City. Observing several meetings between DOE representatives and the members of the community allowed me, in a sense, to retroactively and allo-topographically observe the events leading up to the decision to close The Academy. Considering the intransigence of a symbolic order that relegates Africana and other minority groups to positions of inferiority, animality, and inhumanity, I argue that the closing of a Title I school is the logical fulfillment of a processual project of negation. The constitution of the beings of teachers, students, and administrators of these closing schools is also a fulfillment of this process—they all become "expendable." Furthermore, the high-stakes testing regime, which ensures that school and teaching quality will be inferior, inevitably yields failing scores, which, in the end, provide a scientific justification for why schools must be closed. Arising from the testimonies of community members and in burgeoning lines of inquiry in critical political geography, school closings are taken to be a handmaiden to processes of urban gentrification. Thus, the ultimate conclusion of this chapter is that NCLB, which creates the very conditions for failure, services urban gentrification efforts for the ultimate fulfillment of the chain of signifiers in the symbolic order—the entire community becomes "expendable" and hence non-existent.

The final chapter offers some brief, straightforward recommendations for how we might use an existential psychoanalytic anthropological praxis to revise juridical discourses surrounding education, educational policy, and national systems of educational accountability.

FIELD SUBJECTS

Field Subjects: The Academy, New York City

My field subjects consisted of students, teachers, and administrators. The students were all seventh and eighth graders, between the ages of thirteen and sixteen. They were predominantly black—of African American, Caribbean, and West African origin—and Latina(o)—mainly from Puerto Rico, the Dominican Republic, and various locales in South America. A small minority were Middle Eastern, Asian, or white American. The overwhelming majority of the students lived in neighborhoods and in households that were considered "economically disadvantaged" according to Title I specifications. Many of these students also had significant academic challenges (as evinced by their grades and test scores), learning disabilities, and behavioral challenges. Most of the teachers and administrators were white American. A small minority were Latina(o) and black.

Field Subjects:
Community Elementary School Closing Meetings, New York City

The field subjects consisted mainly of adults, age twenty-five and older. These were parents, community activists, well-wishers, teachers, administrators, and New York City DOE representatives. The overwhelming majority of the parents, community activists, general well-wishers, teachers, and administrators who were in attendance were black Americans, reflecting the demographic of the neighborhood in which Community Elementary School was situated. There was also a small minority of Latina(o) adults present. The representatives, which only numbered between four and six per meeting—were from diverse ethnic backgrounds, which included Latina(o), black, and white.

Duration in the Field

I conducted observations at The Academy for nine consecutive months at irregular intervals. I also attended the Community Elementary school closing meetings at irregular intervals over the course of approximately two months.

DISCUSSION OF METHODOLOGY

The manner by which I entered the field was by no means conventional or easy. My initial strategy involved becoming acquainted with educators to have them lead me to their superiors. For an outside researcher, the task of acquiring a meeting with a principal or lead administrator, however, is virtually impossible in New York City. And, if the research cited up to this point has any merit at all, these barriers were to be expected, as it might prove too dangerous for school leadership to leave their institutions open for any project of active investigation. Needless to say, my proposal was rejected or ignored on numerous occasions. My "break" came when an acquaintance of mine, Joseph Wheeler, a public schoolteacher at The Academy, offered to have me shadow him in his school. Mr. Wheeler happened to have a great deal of power in the school, as he, more than any other teacher, was able to command the respect of the students. Mr. Wheeler's authority proved advantageous for disciplinary and operational issues that the establishment faced. Thus, although the principal, faculty members, and students all knew that I was conducting dissertation research, I was seen as a potential asset rather than as a threat or a distraction to the school. And, indeed, I would prove my utility by doing small "favors" for Mr. Wheeler and other teachers. At times I would make photocopies, gather students into groups for collaborative activities, monitor classrooms while teachers stepped out, or answer academic questions that the students may have asked.

Beyond my practical functionality, it seemed as if I served as a mediator and ad hoc therapist on various occasions. In the school I was generally seen as a warm and agreeable presence. Therefore, when disciplinary issues would arise with students, particularly for teachers who were disliked, my presence was welcome, as I was able to quell tides of hostility that would arise. These situations provided a rich source of ethnographic data, as the troubled students would willingly offer their feelings about the school and whatever situation had been brewing. Teachers, as well, welcomed opportunities to converse with me. Many of them seemed simply to want an opportunity to vent. These venting sessions also proved very fruitful for the collection of informal interview data.

Mr. Wheeler himself was especially generous in mediating my contact with the teachers, students, and administrators on the premises. Because of the favor that he had with the students, for instance, his endorsement of me ensured that students would enter conversations with me willingly and candidly. It was the nature of Mr. Wheeler's endorsement, however, that contributed most to my rapport with the students. He presented me as a strong and accomplished black man who, himself, had emerged from a background similar to their own and made it to the pinnacle of the educational establishment. I was positioned as a role model, an example to follow, and as someone who could help students accomplish their own goals. And I did care for the students, offering advice and words of encouragement whenever appropriate.

I came to conceptualize the "field" in which I was submerged not so much as a flat plane, but rather as a set of concentric spheres: the outermost sphere was New York City itself; the penultimate sphere consisted of the New York City DOE; and the innermost region was The Academy. Because I was living in New York City at the time, I did experience a type of "total" immersion in this outermost sphere, as I was very much attuned to the pulse of the city and the way that debates surrounding education were unfolding at the time. No Child Left Behind and high-stakes testing were hotly debated topics not only in educational circles, but also within the broader New York community. Virtually every week, several articles would appear in local print and television news broadcasts.

Regarding the sphere of the New York City Public School District, as discussed earlier, there were a number of barriers to my gaining access to pedagogical spaces, given the type of research that I wanted to perform. Any possibility of a multi-sited ethnography of various schools, or the inner work-ings of the DOE itself was foreclosed to me at the time.

The possibility of my complete immersion into the sphere of The Acade-my was also hampered by a few intervening obstacles. I was not afforded the luxury of visiting the site every single day, all hours of the school day, as I was working nearly full-time to meet the exigencies of survival and daily life. Certain critical moments, therefore, are conspicuously missing from the ethnographic record. I was able to document the administration of the Eng-lish Language Arts State Examination, for instance, but not the Math State Examination. I was also not able to capture the administration of the State Science Examination (Mr. Wheeler, my primary informant, was the science teacher). Despite these limitations, however, I was able to collect a copious amount of data, enough to establish patterns and draw reasonable conclu-sions, albeit tentative ones.

There was also the inevitable limitation of non-prescience. In my exam-ination of the ethnographic record, having left the field irrevocably, I dis-cerned issues that I wish I could have pursued with follow-up observations. Likewise, as I began to comb through tomes of scholarship from diverse intellectual traditions, issues presented themselves that I regret not having the privilege of pursuing with additional ethnographic observations. Neverthe-less, I consider the astuteness garnered from hindsight not to be a source of regret for having missed several analytic opportunities, but rather a commis-sion for future inquiries. While I cannot help but feel that the present ethnog-raphy is provisional in many ways, I leave the project satisfied that I have laid a solid foundation to further my explorations of existential psychoanalyt-ic anthropology, and existential psychoanalytic anthropology of education more specifically.

Another issue that was a particular source of difficulty was the nature of what I sought to observe. First, I was in pursuit of whom subjects chose to be within a socio-historically defined field. Observing this field meant that I would need to take copious notes regarding the third sphere of immersion, The Academy. Toward this end, I was very attentive to such matters as physical layout, patterns of interaction and exchange, operational function-ing, and customary patterns of behavior.

Second, with respect to the issue of choices of being, the method of collection and the nature of the data itself were more elusive. This situation was to be predicted, as being itself, according to Sartre, is not only elusive, but fundamentally incommensurable with the linguistic register. In other words, it is not possible within a Sartrean framework to access being. Sartre did propose, however, that through an existential psychoanalytic study, one might discover the broad outlines of fundamental projection. This is the juncture at which anthropological theories of consciousness, particularly of cognition and affect, are immensely helpful. Drawing upon the insights of chapter 1, I propose that a hermeneutic analysis of symbols and emotional registers can begin to fill in the broad outlines of fundamental projection and the tropological densities in which students lived. With respect to cognition, for instance, I have sought to understand the ways that the environment of the concentrically configured fieldsite informed the symbolization, semantic systemization, unconscious semiosis, and resonation of the cognitive structures students, teachers, and administrators used to inhabit The Academy on an everyday basis. I also sought to understand the precise ways in which particular structures of affect were related to aspects of the symbolic and the sociocultural field epiphenomenally and comportmentally. In establishing these multiple and crisscrossing lines of connection between context, cognition, and affect, I have undoubtedly deferred to my own cognitive and emotional proclivities, what Bertrand Russell would call "intuition." However, adhering to my own propositions respecting an anthropological theory of consciousness based upon the principle of rigorous intuition, I have grounded my analysis in an elaborate system of data coding, which I will briefly outline.

First, upon leaving the field, I took several months to arrange my notes in ways that facilitated efficient analysis. The entire corpus of notes had already been arranged by date. I continued the process of organization by dividing each page of notes into three arbitrary parts, numbered accordingly. I then worked chronologically through the notes and extracted themes that would be useful for analysis. Next, I created a "Thematized Table of Contents," which is divided by date. Each date is followed by a comprehensive list of themes. Accompanying each theme is the page number on which the theme can be found in the fieldnotes. To the extent possible, I tried to keep the volume of themes to a minimum, both for searchability and more effective delineation of patterns.

In grappling with the phenomenological nature of my data, I also had to attend to how the inevitable differences between my field subjects and me would affect my interpretations. Mark Schroll discusses this very challenge. He states that, historically, there has been an inevitable gulf that has persisted between anthropologists of religion and research subjects. Anthropologists who have studied the religious experiences of shamans, for instance, could only offer a metanarrative for these encounters. He proposed that the new frontier of anthropological methods would be for the researcher to actually inhabit these states of consciousness and be transformed by them (2010). Schroll's proposition is not unlike what Edith Turner experiences in her landmark study of the Congo. In her investigations into the epistemology of religious experience, Turner, unexpectedly, became so immersed within the phenomenological realities of her research subjects that she actually saw a spirit being (1992). While I did inhabit The Academy over the course of nine months and could glean a bit of the texture of how subjects were experiencing their situations, my fundamental difference in social position presented obvious impasses to the types of emic phenomenological breakthrough that Turner experienced. For instance, my age and the fact that I was not enrolled at The Academy prohibited me from truly getting inside the experience of being a student there. Furthermore, because I was not ultimately responsible for these students' pedagogical experiences, I could not truly empathize with the teachers.

Concerning the methodological ideal of emic understanding, educational scholars interested in the field of experience have been particularly gratified by the use of ethnographic methods. For example, in an essay entitled "The Challenge of Urban Ethnography," David M. Smith comments:

> Indeed one of the strengths of ethnography . . . is that it provides a framework for allowing significant problems to arise from the context, to name them and then to locate them in their social context. This cannot be done a priori. (177)

Like Smith, I entered the field with very broadly defined research goals and allowed the field itself to disclose its own possibilities for further inquiry. In fact, my inquiries at The Academy prompted my increasing curiosity into the processes leading up to the closing of schools in urban settings. Because The Academy was already due to close two years from the point at which I had begun my own fieldwork, I could not generate this second line of data from that school. I did, however, seize upon the opportunity to follow the events surrounding the proposition to close a nearby school, Community Elementary School, in the same neighborhood. While I was not permitted to conduct in-school observations of this school, I was able to attend a series of meetings in which New York City DOE representatives interfaced with members of the local community. The data that I collected from these meetings allowed me to retrospectively observe what might have been the events leading up to the closing of The Academy, and of closings occurring all around New York City and urban metropolises nationally. As this project is explicitly concerned with the field of affect, the benefit of observing the events leading up to the time of closing allowed me to see community members' emotional responses to the impending doom of their neighborhood school. In all, I was able to conduct about two months of observations of these meetings.

I must also offer a word about the issue of representativeness. Although the present work is specifically about the disclosure of intersubjective being in The Academy, and, to a lesser extent, Community Elementary School, the governing assumption of this work is that my findings are representative of Title I schools and closing rituals in New York City and urban metropolises across the country. Where appropriate, I corroborate the case for representativeness through relevant research studies.

While educational settings are dynamic, unpredictable fields of intersubjective exchange, they nevertheless provide for more regularity than other potential ethnographic contexts. Like other pedagogical settings, the school day at The Academy at least aspired to some measure of temporal and structural regularity. These regularities often allowed me to easily discern patterns or at least ideal expectations, and consequently, deviations.

Inspired by the recommendations of Russell Bernard (2005), the meticulous manner in which I coded my fieldnotes provided me with at least a modicum of confidence that the cultural patterns that I was perceiving had more than a nominal grounding in the realities of the field.

DISCLAIMER

Regarding my fieldsites, all people and places have been given pseudonyms.

Chapter One

Existential Psychoanalytic Anthropology

What follows is an elaborate exercise in "case-making." My ultimate aim is to make a case for what I have termed "existential psychoanalytic anthropology." Yet, before I make a case for what I envision as the outermost layer of a series of concentric theoretical spheres, I must make a case for each of the interior spheres separately; for each one is indispensable for the integrity of its superior and anterior domain.

I begin with the innermost sphere, where I attempt to understand how mathematics and analytical philosophy achieved credibility as positivist sciences, despite having no empirical substrate. Even more curious is that in the writings of Bertrand Russell, a pioneer in the philosophy of mathematics, analytical philosophy, and logical positivism more broadly, is that he admits that a governing intuition, not truth or an empirical object, must be the inevitable starting point for the mathematical and logical systems that he encodes. If intuition be at the helm of logical positivism, then how is it that so many philosophers, social scientists, physiologists, and behavioral scientists can accept the validity of mathematics and analytical philosophy, yet disavow the validity of consciousness either as a stable object of inquiry or a source of truth claim validation? I argue that the continued ascendance of logical positivism is a result of a particular operation, whereby the "rigour" (Bertrand Russell's term) of systematicity displaces "intuition" as the foundation for making claims of scientific validity. This fundamental displacement, I argue in subsequent sections, accounts, in part, for the many difficulties that attend the development of a rigorous science of consciousness generally, and an anthropological theory of consciousness in particular. I regard this first exposition as "clearing the way" for the possibility of a science of consciousness.

I continue to clear the way in the second sphere, in which I discuss the many impediments to having an anthropological theory of consciousness. I reference four primary challenges. First, I explore the tendency in analytical philosophy to agnostically disregard the very existence of consciousness and its variegated contents. Second, I argue that one significant challenge to the goal in question is anthropology's aversion to grand theorizing. This aversion, I argue, is the product of the Boasian legacy of cultural particularism and anthropology's guilt surrounding complicity with the colonial enterprise. Third, there is the nebulousness of consciousness itself. The term itself is a composite of cognition, affect, and perceptual sensation. To have a science of something that is essentially composite inevitably creates a crisis of operationalization. Compounding the nebulousness of consciousness is also the nebulous ontology of anthropology itself. Unlike the disciplines of history, political science, and literature, for instance, which include their ontic material within their ontological brands (e.g., the field of literature has an empirically observable entity, the name of which is consonant with its encompassing area of study: literature), anthropology has no such object. One cannot go into the world and see anthropology. The proliferation of subspecies of the discipline contributes enormously to this sense of ontological nebulosity. The fourth impediment is that anthropology has a disciplinary charter on culture, which is itself an ontological composite that includes consciousness. Thus, not only must anthropology distill consciousness (an operationalized consciousness) from the diverse mass of items that make up culture, it must also lay disciplinary ownership to consciousness, which historically has been the property of psychology, physiology, and philosophy. Once all four impediments are disarmed, then an anthropological theory of consciousness is possible. I argue that anthropology is especially suited to offer a theory of consciousness that has transdisciplinary credibility for the following reason: although philosophy and various branches of psychology have offered many compelling theories of human consciousness, anthropology, over three centuries and within diverse human locales, has been uniquely positioned to test and revise these theories, as well as pioneer new ones. Furthermore, I argue that several consolidated theories of consciousness have always been anthropology's disciplinary charter, originating particularly in studies of religion, ritual, symbols, and linguistics. Many of these theories have simply not been foregrounded and consolidated due to the four impediments previously described. What I attempt to do is excavate some theoretical propositions regarding cognition and affect from the preponderance of anthropological material; I do not take on perceptual sensation, as someone with a more extensive knowledge of neurophysiology would be better suited for this task.

I am now led to the third sphere: here I make the case for distinctively anthropological insights regarding cognition and affect. I am particularly interested in distilling the "mechanisms" of cognition and emotion. For cognition, I define four key mechanisms: symbolization, systemization, unconscious semiosis, and resonation. All four are based on the anthropological insight that cognition proceeds through the accretion and systematic arrangement of both conscious and unconscious meanings, all of which have the power to profoundly affect structures of thought (in a feedback loop), emotion, physiology, and culture. For affect I outline two: epiphenomenality and comportmentality. The first regards emotion as the epiphenomenal emanation of existential circumstance, while the second refers to emotion as the manner by which individuals comport themselves to exist within these circumstances. In this section, I also offer some brief methodological recommendations for how these elements of cognition and affect can be recovered and studied in the field.

In the fourth sphere, I consider Sartre's theories of consciousness, good faith, bad faith, existential psychoanalysis, and fundamental projection/ fundamental choice. There are two parts to this discussion. First, I consider only Sartre and offer novel insights concerning his meditations upon the French Occupation of Germany. For Sartre, being is a consequence of a fundamental choice among culturally and historically determined possibles that one makes of whom he or she will become. This fundamental choice is compelling, yet largely inaccessible, and sets the tone for all subsequent experiences. Through an analysis of Sartre's French Occupation journals, I advance the notion that configurations of tropes are the dense particles of these experiences. I call these particles "tropological densities." I go on to extend Sartre's insights regarding consciousness and fundamental projection in particular, using various thinkers in the African existentialist tradition. I evoke this tradition for two reasons: (1) Some of these thinkers have either dealt directly with Sartre or some of the themes that emerge from Sartre's work; (2) Africana thought and where Africana people fit within the symbolic order are particularly germane to my fieldsites. In this section, I show how the Africana existentialist tradition allows us to not only see fundamental projection as individual and hermetic, but also intersubjective. In showing us that the fundamental projects of Africana peoples have been forged in intersubjective encounters between blackness and whiteness, thinkers such as Gordon, Yancy, and Mbembe help us see that Sartre's insights are applicable to the sociocultural with which anthropologists primarily deal.

The fifth sphere simply consolidates the other four to articulate the possibility for an existential psychoanalytic anthropology.

THE RIGOROUSLY INTUITIVE DISPLACEMENT OF INTUITION FOR RIGOR

I am not here interested in performing a critique of positivism. This task has been accomplished in both Continental and analytical philosophy, the humanities more broadly, and the social sciences. I have no abiding fascination with exposing the contradiction, hypocrisy, and brutality of such modes of study, but rather the mechanisms through which positivistic inquiry achieves its particular brand of cultural preeminence. At this point I must evoke a distinction that Weinberg makes in *An Examination of Logical Positivism* (1936) between scientific positivism and logical positivism. Many are well aware of the arguments for and against various applications of the former. Proponents tout the human benefits of electricity, telecommunication, intercontinental transport, epidemiology, and a comprehensive understanding of how our physical universe is constituted. Opponents, particularly those in various branches of the social sciences and humanities, sneer at the ineffectual nature of hypothetico-deductive models for explaining such phenomena as human creativity, social change, religious fervor, or mentation itself. It is logical positivism, which has obvious genealogical ties to its sister discipline, that is of particular interest for the present study.

While guilty of the same errors for which scientific positivists reject metaphysics, logical positivism remains somehow unscathed in disciplinary frays (both within disciplines and between them) over methodology. Such a glaring contradiction warrants an explanation. Let us turn first to the matter of logical positivism.

In the textbook account of logical positivism, the discipline emerged as a virulent reaction to metaphysics, the origins of which are often traced to Aristotle. According to Michael Loux, Aristotelian metaphysics was chiefly concerned with two types of contemplative inquiries: (1) proving the existence of an Unmoved Mover and (2) studying being *qua* being (1998). The first of these, which is tantamount to proving the existence of God, has obviously been the more controversial of the two in all subfields of philosophy. For, Aristotle was essentially positing an entity that is beyond the physical realm of all that humans can empirically verify and yet somehow the source of that very realm. Aristotle was engaged in the seemingly impossible task of lending veracity to that which is fundamentally immaterial. His study of being was almost as arcane, yet only slightly less objectionable. He framed metaphysics as a universal science that studied being itself by identifying the highest level categories into which all existents fall. The task of the metaphysician then is to provide a categorial map of all that there is.

Aristotle intended for these categories, however, to correspond to a pre-philosophical understanding of the world (Loux 1998). The most elemental categories, for instance, would consist of ideal types that were naturally occurring in the geosphere—a caterpillar or a lake, for instance. Yet, in the seventeenth and eighteenth centuries, there emerged a new variety of metaphysicians whose "maps" of being became progressively more alien from commonsense understandings of the world. It was these abstract inquiries into being that empiricists, who insisted that all propositions be legitimated through sense experience, rejected. If the disjunction between experiential common sense and logical propositions, and the preoccupation with the immaterial define the positivist reaction against metaphysics, it becomes quite fascinating how logical positivism negotiates its own relation to those immaterialities that define its particular enterprise, namely logical and mathematical systems. A brief examination of Bertrand Russell's effort to align logical and mathematical philosophy provides an illustrative example of this type of negotiation.

Weinberg (1936) argues that the development of logic was singularly responsible for the rise of present "positivistic tendencies," and that it was the ideas of Frege and Russell that lent to logical positivism its formal methodology (11). While the culmination of these efforts was Russell's magisterial *Principia Mathematica* in 1910, a concise formulation of that work's major premises arrived in 1919 when Russell published *Introduction to Mathematical Philosophy* (2005). I will focus on the latter work, as it contains statements particularly salient to the present exposition of logical positivism's relation to the immaterial. The aim of *Introduction* was to: (a) distill the small set of premises on which mathematics has been established (a procedure that is necessarily retroactive); and (b) to derive from these premises all of mathematics and the latter's corollary: a self-contained system of logical symbology.

In his derivational project, Russell begins with a concept considered to be foundational to all mathematical systems: the series of natural numbers (represented by 1, 2, 3, 4 . . . n, n+1, and on to infinity). Despite the status of natural numbers as foundational, because they are abstractions from more provincial and antiquated constructions of quantity (e.g., a score for the number 20 or a brace for the number 2), Russell considers them to represent a relatively advanced stage of mathematical sophistication. Even more current, and hence, "advanced," in Russell's typology is the number 0, which postdates Greek and Roman civilizations. If 0 and the series of natural numbers are to constitute a point of origin for Russell, then he must lend to them the concreteness of definitions. Otherwise, there can be no foundation at all. Alas, however, he concedes that no definition of these items is even possible given that all terms must be reducible to others in an infinite regression of derived meanings. He then moves to what could be interpreted as either an induction from the foregoing statement or a proposition from which that statement had been deduced: "It is clear that human knowledge must always be content to accept some terms as intelligible without definition, in order to have a starting-point for its definitions" (3). From the void of indefinability, the natural numbers become extant, axiomatic, and foundational all at once. In other words, the conferral of these properties is but an act of arbitration.

What occurs next is quite remarkable. Russell states:

> All traditional pure mathematics, including analytical geometry, may be regarded as consisting wholly of propositions about the natural numbers. That is to say, the terms which occur can be defined by means of the natural numbers, and the propositions can be deduced from the properties of the natural numbers—with the addition, in each case, of the ideas and propositions of pure logic. (3–4)

The admission that mathematics, logic, and the composite operations of *Introduction* are essentially founded upon nothingness with an arbitrarily conferred existence is almost Sartrean. Despite the paradoxical, conferred origins of mathematics, Russell proceeds to name the set of premises and undefined terms upon which a theory of the natural numbers could be founded. He evokes the mathematician Peano, who identified "three primitive ideas"—"0," "number," and "successor"—and "five primitive propositions"—(1) 0 is a number; (2) The successor of any number is a number; (3) No two numbers have the same successor; (4) 0 is not the successor of any number; (5) Any property which belongs to 0, and also to the successor of every number which has the property, belongs to all numbers.

Regarding Peano's three primitive ideas, he says:

> We know what we mean by "0" and "number" and "successor," though we cannot explain what we *mean* [my emphasis] in terms of other simpler concepts. It is quite legitimate to say this when we must, and at *some* [Russell's emphasis] point we all must; but it is the object of mathematical philosophy to put off saying it as long as possible. (8)

The *meaning* of the three primitive ideas (like the meaning of natural numbers), ascertainable without subsequent regressions in definition, amounts to an intuition of the sense of things. And, although we may delay the admission that we need the intuition, we "must" eventually make this very concession. It appears that Russell wanted to do more than delay this admission, however; he wanted to eliminate it altogether. In the chapter entitled "Incompatibility and the Theory of Deduction" he explains that Kant invented a theory of mathematical reasoning in which inferences were never purely logical, but would always require an intuition. Russell admonishes that no mathematical system can rely upon common sense or intuition, but must advance through strict, logical deduction from premises. It is this latter objective that Russell named "rigour" (130–131). I am inclined to interpret the discrepancy between Russell's initial concession to intuition and his subsequent rejection of it not as a contradiction, however; the disjuncture would be more accurately termed a substitution, or rather a displacement. In a moment of arbitration equally as willful as the axiomatic establishment of natural numbers, the rigor of mathematical deduction displaces intuition as a means of verification and discernment of the sense of things.

Once the principle of intuition is replaced by that of rigor, only one more stage of development is required for mathematical systems to be constructed: the five primitive propositions which were mentioned earlier. It is the fifth of these—any property which belongs to 0, and also to the successor of every number which has the property, belongs to all numbers—that Russell considers the launching point for all mathematical induction. For, it is this proposition that confers a measure of certitude in the existence of any number that results from any mathematical operation, even if there is no empirically observed correlate to that number in the extant universe. The concept of infinity itself serves as a concise illustration of this theme. Based on Peano's propositions, natural numbers repeat into infinity, although it is impossible to directly observe the totality of all that has and will exist. Yet, the concept itself not only has a linguistic value ("infinity") and a pictorial one (∞), but it also has a numerical/algebraic one as well: $1, 2, 3, 4 \ldots n, n+1 \ldots$. It is these numerical/algebraic representations that Russell and other logicians—most notably, his student Wittgenstein—deem superior to the other two. What is most notable for our purposes, however, is that the preeminence of this numerical/algebraic representation is a function of the following five-part procedure: (a) an intuition makes the three primitive ideas and five primitive propositions tenable; (b) intuition is rendered imperfect, yet necessary to the goal of having a mathematical system; (c) mathematical systems are elaborated as if their foundations were perfectly stable; (d) as a foundation for these mathematical systems, intuition is deemed unstable and antithetical to the goal of mathematical deduction itself; finally, (e) rigor, the principle by which mathematical propositions are logically deduced from others, anachronistically replaces intuition as the foundation for mathematics.

With the substitution of intuition for rigor, logical deduction becomes the cardinal virtue of mathematics. Having completed this procedure, Russell is able to elaborate the system of logic that undergirds mathematics. In fact, one of Russell's ultimate conclusions in *Introduction* as well as *Principia* is that all of mathematics is reducible to logic, and, even further, that the two are indistinguishable (refer to the chapter in *Introduction* entitled "Mathematics and Logic" for a full exposition of this argument). Despite aligning mathematics and logic, Russell does imply that logic is the more fundamental of the two. Russell, like his predecessors, contended that an entire logical symbology could be delineated, and that within this system any deduction whatsoever could be framed. This symbology had to exist as a specialized system apart from language, however, as Russell—like Wittgenstein, Leibniz, and others—considered language to be riddled with imprecision and ambiguity (Russell, 185). However, the procedure through which mathematical syntax derives its initial legitimacy from a founding intuition mirrors that through which Russell's logical syntax achieves its preeminence through language.

For example, in "Mathematics and Logic," Russell is attempting to derive a "pure" system of logic. In such a system, the particular objects in the world about which logical propositions can be made would not be a requirement for the logical forms of the propositions themselves. Yet, just as the enumeration of the founding propositions of mathematics began with a consideration of natural numbers and the intuitions that made these intelligible, so the enumeration of logical principles begins in language-bound propositions about empirically observable entities. Russell illustrates this point with a proposition about the relation between Socrates and Aristotle: "Socrates was before Aristotle." He distills from this particular proposition the pure form of "x R y," asserting that each of the form's constituent parts may be legitimately substituted (i.e., Monday comes before Tuesday, or strawberries are more sour than coconuts). Stated another way, x R y represents the logical structure of all propositions expressing the aforementioned type of relation. Analogous to the infinite set of all natural numbers discussed earlier (1, 2, 3, 4 . . . n, n+1), that all the entities that could possibly have the relation x R y are not verifiable through sense experience does not undermine the legitimacy of that logical structure and the forms that express them. Russell states: "We are left with pure forms as the only possible constituents of logical propositions" (179). The assemblage of these forms thus constitutes an autonomous system, free from the encumbrances of objects in the world and the ambiguities of language.

Yet, despite the procedure whereby Russell distills the pure forms of logic, there remains the adumbration of that which would threaten to compromise the entire procedure. He states, "Logical propositions are such as can be known *a priori*, without study of the actual world" (184). In other words, the sensibleness of logical propositions presents itself to consciousness as immediate, ineffable (i.e., unmediated by language) revelations of truth. If this be the case, then such knowledge must be absolutely reliant upon intuition—an intuition that somehow circumvents sense experience. As with the displacement previously described concerning mathematical systems, it appears that an analogous one has occurred in the establishment of logical deduction: (a) sense observation provides the necessary basis for establishing logical syntax; (b) the world is then discounted as a necessary and sufficient condition for the establishment of a logical syntax; (c) the pure syntactical forms become an autonomous system; (d) syntax replaces sense observation as the basis of logical deduction; and finally, (e) in displacing sense experience as the vehicle through which one may confirm logical propositions, logical syntax (an additional manifestation of "rigour") displaces intuition.

If the symbolic systems of logic and mathematics have as their point of origin intuition and common sense, how have these systems managed to become the exemplars of positivism, and the antithesis of metaphysics? Furthermore, how have these systems become synonymous with "rigour" to the exclusion of intuition—in analytical philosophy and the social sciences alike—when rigor itself would not even have been possible without intuition? As the foregoing discussion demonstrates, logic and mathematics have achieved their positions through very particular strategies of displacement, disavowing the very features on which they necessarily depend, replacing these with elaborate syntactical structures. It is one of my contentions that the systems' complexity and autonomy—as textually inscribed and promulgated arrangements—provide the ossified contours of their ontological structures. As a corollary to this claim, I would also argue that because the intuitive and the commonsensical, at least in the historical moment here named, had no such ontological structure to rival those of logic and mathematics, the former two were almost guaranteed to be usurped in cultural and intellectual preeminence. If the intuitive sense of things—the structures of consciousness—be the repressed metaphysical origin of positivism, and if all agree that the positivist enterprise would be more useful to the aims of social science if it would simply amend itself to include other methodologies, then would not a "rigorous" engagement with metaphysics—particularly, a metaphysics of consciousness—be a welcome paradigm shift, particularly within cultural anthropology?

I began this section with the disclaimer that I have no intention of diminishing the importance of logical positivism. For, without it, anthropology would not have any grounding at all. Understanding the ways in which culture shapes human existence, for instance, requires an assent to a positivistic approach. And, anthropology has developed quite rigorous positivistic methodologies. One need only consult such disciplinary hallmarks as kinship, structural-functionalism, participant-observation, and biocultural evolution to confirm the truth of this statement. Yet, due to the ascendancy of positivism in anthropological discourse and the social sciences more broadly, I would argue, methodologies of a more metaphysical nature have remained in their infancy. Even those methodologies that are hybrids of metaphysical and positivistic approaches tend to leave the metaphysical half underdeveloped. Rather than replacing intuition with rigor, it is necessary to acknowledge that the latter is and has always been nothing more than a particular interpretation of the former. For this reason, I am advocating not simply a return to metaphysics, at least as it has been understood in philosophy and the social sciences, but rather a procedure by which the metaphysical center of positivism is acknowledged, legitimized, and methodologically codified. Just as logical positivism has achieved preeminence through a series of discursive strategies, so must an anthropological metaphysics of consciousness establish itself through a rigorous systematicity. Understood another way, I am arguing for an anthropological method that achieves systematic rigour (in Russell's sense of the word) in propositions concerning human consciousness. Anthropology is the ideal discursive field for such an enterprise; for, in contradistinction to logical positivism, the discipline has always insisted upon the inseverability of theoretical systems and the cultural worlds that provide the conditions of these systems' possibility. What I have sought to achieve in the foregoing section is simply to create an opening for an anthropological metaphysics of consciousness. In the following section I continue to widen this opening by examining additional challenges to formulating a rigorous anthropological theory of consciousness.

CHALLENGES TO AN ANTHROPOLOGICAL
THEORY OF CONSCIOUSNESS

1. Philosophy's Ambiguous Treatment of Consciousness as a Site of Inquiry

Logical positivism's displacement of intuition is a symptom of positivist philosophy's skepticism concerning the very existence of consciousness. According to George Shields, analytical philosophy of mind has tended to declaim the relevance, even existence of consciousness. Shields illustrates his point with a brief discussion of Carl Hempel's stimulus-response model (S-R), a logical behaviorism that reduces all claims about mental activity to logical propositions about external behavior (Shields 2012). Psychology and neuroscience have also succumbed to this reductionism born of skepticism. Psychology has tended to reduce consciousness to behavior, while neuroscience has reduced it to the neural dynamics of the brain (Zahavi 2007). However, whether through substitution, disavowal, or existential negation, the refusal to deal with the "hard problem of consciousness," though popular, is by no means universal.

Philosophers Searle (1994) and Whitehead (1978) regard the materialist elimination of consciousness as ensuring a descent into absurdity. Both concur that such a procedure is simply inconsistent with the ways in which human beings experience. One solution to materialist tendencies has been to lend an ontological structure to consciousness. Keith Lehrer makes such an ambitious attempt in his theory of exemplarization, the phenomenon whereby humans represent experience to themselves (Studenberg 2012). Lehrer regards this self-referential mechanism as the very substance of experience itself (Lehrer 2006).

Within the philosophical tradition, Husserl is regarded as the most prominent figure to not only attempt to establish the existence of the mind, but to develop a rigorous methodology for studying it. Husserl's entire agenda was to understand the mechanisms through which the mind allows us to know the world.[1] According to Husserl, while going about our everyday affairs, we do not achieve this degree of insight into our own consciousness, for we exist primarily in the "natural attitude." The job of the phenomenologist, therefore, is to disfigure the natural attitude—a phenomenon that Husserl calls "bracketing"—thereby becoming reflectively attuned to the ways in which our minds come to know the world. And, because consciousness is "intentional," always reaching out to something else (Sartre framed it thus: consciousness is always consciousness of something[2]), bracketing provides insight into the mechanisms of the mind and the world simultaneously and indissociably[3] (Overgaard 2008). In sum, Husserlian phenomenology maintains the inextricability of mind and world; disclosing the structures of mind, therefore, invariably will reveal the world.

In reading Husserl and others in phenomenological philosophy, then, one confronts a few dilemmas—dilemmas particularly resonant for anthropology. First, phenomenologists such as Hegel, Husserl, Sartre, Heidegger, and Merleu-Ponty—though there are immense differences between them—all base their thinking on the premise that the minds of all human beings have a universal ontological structure. Yet, if we accept the conclusion of many phenomenologists that consciousness and the world are an indissociable totality, then would not different types of habitations of the world—that is, different experiences—induce a proliferation of consciousnesses? How is one to resolve the seeming antinomy—the coexistence of humankind's psychic unity and the experience-laden proliferation of mind—that emerges from within the phenomenological project? And, if such an antinomy persists, would it ever be possible to construct a "rigorous" science of consciousness, especially if that science insists upon its ability to make general claims about all of humanity? It is my contention that anthropology has provided some useful, and in many respects, definitive, answers to these and related questions. Moreover, I would argue that a proto-theory of consciousness has already been elaborated; it only need be consolidated and codified. Yet first, it is worth explaining why no such theory has entered forcefully into the broad field of trans-disciplinary understandings.

2. Anthropology's Aversion to Grand Theorizing

Laypeople and intellectuals (present company excluded) never look to anthropology for a theory of consciousness—how the mind works, how humans experience the world, or some other such framing. As Geertz suggested in the incipient essay to *Interpretation of Cultures*, academic disciplines tend to be defined by what they "do." He continues by asserting that, for anthropology, this practical activity has involved "ethnography," the gloss of which I take to be "fieldwork" (1973). Thus, the world continues to depend upon anthropology only to furnish the results of nineteenth- and early-twentieth-century–styled fieldwork expeditions to remote corners of the world.[4] Anthropology, at least the sociocultural variety, is the patron saint of "thick" cultural descriptions—of kinships maps, elaborate social network schemes, cultural genealogies, religious rites, tribal forms of government, and primeval systems of monetary exchange. That anthropology might contribute profoundly to our understanding of such fields as politics, psychology, and economics is as foreign of an idea as the stereotypical objects of anthropological investigation. Moreover, that anthropology could make valuable contributions to that elite corpus of theories that transcend and suffuse all social science and humanities disciplines is not even considered as a possibility. On the world intellectual stage, no one seems to be aware that what anthropologists "do," and have always done, is much more substantial than simply cataloging customs, rites, and social systems. I would argue that one of the grandest accomplishments of the discipline is that, for at least a century, it has been elaborating many robust insights regarding consciousness. Yet, the academic community's ignorance of this fact is partly the fault of anthropologists themselves.

Let us consider Boas's seminal contribution to the establishment of the discipline in the United States. By the late nineteenth and early twentieth centuries, the systematic "study of humankind" had already become entangled with evolutionism. Spencer, Morgan, and Tylor had all ensured that humankind would be arranged along a continuum that runs from simple to advanced societies. With this neo-Darwinian scheme intact, anthropology was poised to make a discipline-specific contribution to the coveted domain of social and humanistic metatheory: the linear evolution of human beings and human societies. As a result of this focus, from its very emergence in the United States, anthropology espoused the idea that there were scientific laws guiding the progression of human beings and the societies into which they were arranged. The anthropologist, therefore, was responsible for discovering and explicating these laws. Although Boas maintained his allegiance to this disciplinary charter early on in his career, he frequently wavered in his opinion, and eventually dealt, what came to be the definitive blow to the evolutionist scheme. Skeptical about our ability to make generic claims that could be applied to all cultures of the world, Boas insisted that anthropology focus its energies upon studying each culture in its particularity (Stocking 1992). The undermining of social evolutionism was, indeed, necessary, as this paradigm was directly implicated in racist, sexist and classist regimes of power. Furthermore, the undoing of evolutionism was critical to the integrity of the discipline itself. For, how could a discipline exist under the umbrella of the humanities—which is invested in enriching human lives—and the social sciences—which studies human societies for the sake of improving them—if its foundation runs counter to the agendas of both? As matters of both logic and disciplinary ethics, it was virtually impossible (thankfully so) for anthropology to maintain its alliance with nineteenth-century evolution-ism.

Yet, in the wake of evolutionism (although it is not often acknowledged that anthropology has outgrown this way of thinking), the continued ascen-dance of Boas's cultural particularism and its corollary—anthropologists' confessional, guilt-ridden, compulsory avoidance of grand theorizing—how will anthropology assume its rightful place on the world stage of theory? Can the discipline forgive itself for its past inhumanity, so that it may offer grand theories without being charged with complicity in the colonial enterprise? Undoubtedly, one of anthropology's greatest contributions to the post-modern era has been cultural relativism, thanks to Boas (1940), Hurston (1990), Mead (2001), and many others. Due partly to this pioneering idea, people in the world are well on their way to a more truly democratic way of perceiving and living with one another. On the academic front, the relativist model has made for a generation of scholars who are more open to the idea that difference does not imply hierarchy. In addition to cultural relativism, the ethnographic method has had a most felicitous welcome in the integrated fields of psychotherapy, education, and mostly all of the social sciences; for these fields know that, in order to understand and make claims about people, one must actually speak to them and see how they live on an everyday basis. In short, cultural relativism and ethnography have had a profound influence upon what scholars "do" and how they do it.

Yet, while anthropology continues to make its interdisciplinary mark with respect to how research is done, we have not achieved this same currency with regard to the products of research. Said another way, anthropology's presence is felt much more palpably in the realm of methodology than theory. The question naturally would arise, therefore: Has anthropology birthed any theories worth trans-disciplinary inclusion? Of course, I have already stated my position to be affirmative, particularly with regard to theo-ries of consciousness. What is interesting about the elaboration of these theories, however, is that, historically, they have asserted themselves through relativistic negation. In other words, by eschewing nomothetic explanations of culture and human consciousness, thus insisting upon the uniqueness of each culture[5] and the minds contained within them, anthropology has ad-vanced some quite astute theories of consciousness. It is to this matter that I now turn in earnest.

3. The Nebulous Ontology of Consciousness and the Discipline of Anthropology

Compounding the difficulties previously stated, one major impediment to the achievement of definitive anthropological theories of consciousness has been the nebulousness of the very concept of consciousness itself. Now, many times, when an appeal is made to a dictionary, only an apocryphal sense of legitimation is achieved, analogy masquerading as causality. If we assume, however, that the science of lexicography both captures and institutes modes of reasoning and symbolization in a cultural group, and we are attempting to illuminate one such connection, then an appeal to dictionaries is completely warranted. Such is the case with the notion of consciousness. Merriam-Webster's dictionary defines the term thus: "the state of being characterized by sensation, emotion, volition, and thought: mind" (2014). One sees immediately the challenge. The potential explanatory power of a concept for the sciences and the social sciences has always been that concept's amenability to narrow operationalizing, a sort of commonsense simplicity, if you will. The problem with consciousness is that, as a concept, it includes physical sensation, cognition (I am eliding volition and thought), and emotion. Well, in the popular and scholarly imagination, all three not only represent completely different categories of experience, but each has already been claimed by a well-established field of study: medicine has claimed physical sensation, and psychology has done so with mentation and emotion. One could argue that philosophy is the home of consciousness. After all, one could site a long genealogy, ranging from Aristotle through Husserl and Heidegger, to buttress this claim. However, the psychologist, psychotherapist and the psychoanalyst each has an equally legitimate charter on consciousness, at least by the very logic through which these common associations often emerge and endure. Because of the composite nature of consciousness, it is owned by no one. So, why should it be given to the anthropologist? Such a gesture would be tantamount to bequeathing poetry to the historian rather than the literary scholar, or language to the sociologist rather than the linguist.

Even further prohibiting a distinctly anthropological theory of consciousness is the ontic status of the discipline. Like philosophy, anthropology lacks ontic being in the real world. Literature, history, politics, and economics, by contrast, are not only fields of study, but fields of study that have correlating ontic objects in the realm of lived experience: one can purchase literature, live within a distinct historical period, be subjugated by political dominance, and participate in an economy; there are quite lucid resemblances between these fields and the objects constituting them. The solidity of these fields of knowledge is reflected in their grammatical constitution. They are almost invariably referenced as subjective (grammatical, not personal subjectivity) nouns, while their many iterations inhabits the position of adjectival modifiers (e.g., twentieth-century literature, ancient Sumerian history, Marxist economics, and South African politics). Anthropology has no such ontology or system of resemblances. Therefore, the grammar of the discipline is quite different. The many iterations of anthropology are attended by modifiers just the same, yet the latter are frequently prepositional. Thus, we get "anthropology of gender," "anthropology of race," and so forth. The discipline is treated much more as an approach, a heuristic or a methodology, than an ontically bound field of investigation. The prepositional objects, predictably, function as the solid objects of study. Sure, one might cite "medical anthropology" and "psychological anthropology" as evidence of a counterclaim to the aforementioned argument. However, it is virtually undeniable that the sub-disciplines of anthropology have been enumerated predominately as prepositional objects.

Enter now "anthropology of consciousness." Anthropology is the method and consciousness is the object; only, the object itself, due to its operational deficiencies and ambiguities, and due to the positivist assault on its very existence and legitimacy, is not very solid. And within anthropology of consciousness or perhaps related to it only laterally (I believe this matter is unresolved), are anthropology of affect, anthropology of experience (which includes the anthropology of embodiment), existential anthropology (which, at times is indistinguishable from the anthropology of experience), cognitive anthropology, psychological anthropology, transpersonal anthropology, psychoanalytic anthropology, symbolic anthropology, and phenomenological anthropology. Within this confounding profusion, operational variables are virtually impossible to distill; and, if consciousness cannot be operationalized, then it would appear that no theory of consciousness is even possible. Yet despite the formidability of the task, I remain convinced that, not only is some consolidated theory of consciousness worth pursuing, but also that its rudiments have already achieved ontic solidity, at least within the discipline. And, to reiterate a point made earlier, anthropology is uniquely qualified to proffer such a theory to the elite realm of trans- and interdisciplinary meta-theory.

4. Anthropology's Charter on Culture and the Problem of Distilling Consciousness from Culture

Up to this point, I have been explaining the features of the discipline that have proven inhospitable to the goal of operationalizing and distilling the component parts of consciousness. A final feature must be considered before proceeding to the goal itself. An anthropological theory of consciousness has been largely hampered by the privileged position of "culture," which itself already includes consciousness. It is apparent to me that Tylor's definition has not lost its currency today. One might cite, for instance, Michael Jackson's contributions to the existentialist and phenomenological movements in anthropology. In his introduction to the volume of collected essays, *Lifeworlds: Essays in Existential Anthropology*, Jackson argues that a phenomenological anthropology must take as its object, the "lifeworld," or the irreducible "flux" of experience (2012). While *Lifeworlds* and some of Jackson's other work (Jackson 2002, 2005) foreground consciousness much more emphatically than does Tylor's work, what Jackson calls the "lifeworld," which is synonymous with experience, is virtually indistinguishable from Tylor's seminal pronouncement in *Primitive Culture* that culture is "that complex whole which includes knowledge, belief, art, law, morals, customs, and any other capabilities and habits acquired by man as a member of society" (1871). Jackson even cites Tylor's definition of culture as an important source of the lifeworld concept (17).

Indeed, "culture" is the cardinal rule of sociocultural anthropology, and justifiably so. In fact, the many profusions of anthropology mentioned earlier have originated by this very insistence upon the explanatory virtues of culture. In medical anthropology, for example, culture explains the social causes of illness and the ways these illnesses are lived (Lee et al. 2007, Davies 2011, Grinker and Cho 2013, Kirmayer 2008, Csordas 1994, Mimica 2007, Watson-Gegeo 2011, Throop 2012, Lende and Downey 2012). In black queer anthropology, culture accounts for how queerness is constituted and manifested in African Diasporic cultures (Allen 2011, McGlotten 2012, Gill 2012). In the anthropology of affect, culture is taken to be productive of and produced by specific emotional forms (Epstein 1992, Clarke 2011, Hollan 2008, Lutz and White 1986, Charlesworth 2005). Finally, one of the most compelling examples of culture's explanatory power occurred in Edith Turner's ethnography, *Experiencing Ritual: A New Interpretation of African Healing*, when, after spontaneously witnessing a spirit during her fieldwork in Zambia, the author attributed the experience to having been immersed in the cultural life of the Ndembu people (1992).

In sum, anthropology has consistently nominated culture itself as the operational value, regardless of the object of investigation. This fact makes the distillation of consciousness from the composite mass of culture that much more complicated, and also poses great difficulties for the operationalizing of consciousness. I am not here arguing that we relinquish our charter on culture; for, we all know that to do such a thing would ensure the collapse of the discipline. Instead, I am arguing that, if we are to advance a distinctly anthropological theory of consciousness, then we must, within the composite of culture, allow consciousness to be buoyed to the surface. Yet the surfacing of consciousness still does not resolve the composite and amorphous nature of this conceptual juggernaut. Anthropologists of experience have been reluctant to disaggregate consciousness into what Merriam-Webster takes to be its component parts—cognition, emotion, and bodily sensation. For, the triad obviously constitutes an interdependent, dynamic integrity. As Jackson states, corroborating a point made by Adorno, "Attempting to cover or contain the flux of experience with finite, all-encompassing, and bounded terms is seen to be absurd" (2012). Despite the "absurdity" of such isolationism, disaggregation has had remarkable results for the trans-disciplinary influence of Turner's theories of ritual, liminality, and performance; Levi-Strauss's structuralism; and Durkheim's work on ritual, religion, and social formations, for instance. And, of course, contributing to the wide circulation of these various authors' ideas is the fact that grand theories frequently are an open invitation for debate and caviling. If anthropology is to offer the world a compelling theory of consciousness, rhetorical isolation, not ontic (as this procedure would be truly absurd), is essential. I have already distilled consciousness from culture. It now would serve us to continue by de-synthesizing consciousness. It only makes sense to accomplish this feat by taking as foundational the triad of cognition, emotion, and bodily sensation.

For the present study, I will focus on cognition and emotion. With the final concept—which indexes the incontrovertibly embodied nature of the first two, and provides the nexus between humans and culture—I will not have any comprehensive dealings. Two issues inform my decision. First, such a treatment—if it is to have trans-disciplinary merit—requires an extensive knowledge of the body, particularly the nervous system, which is the seat of experience. This corpus of knowledge transcends my field of expertise. There is a great deal of stellar work being done on this front in neuro-anthropology, however (see Lende and Downey 2012, Laughlin 1990, Throop and Laughlin 2009). Second, among neuroanthropology, anthropology of embodiment, and medical anthropology, I feel that the body, particularly its connection to the mind and experience, is already well on its way to fulfilling its potential as a consolidated theoretical domain. Anthropological theories of cognition and emotion are in more urgent need of elaboration. Despite the omission of the sensual/bodily in the following discussion, these elements will certainly figure into the ethnographic chapters.

AN ANTHROPOLOGICAL THEORY OF COGNITION

By now it should be apparent that the difficulty of advancing an anthropological theory of cognition is that, historically, cognition has been embedded within more encompassing theories of culture. Therefore, to construct a theory of consciousness requires a bit of excavation in some instances, synthesizing in others, and renaming in still others. I am not so much concerned with identifying subdisciplinary origins of ideas (i.e., whether a certain idea originates from the phenomenological or the structuralist school, for example), as I am the functional utility of the ideas themselves. For, as we know, anthropological concepts inhabit myriad subdisciplines at once. The defining question for this pursuit is: "What are the mechanisms of consciousness?" When considering how this question illuminates our understanding of each member of the triad, one need only substitute the final term. For the immediate inquiry then, the question becomes: "What are the mechanisms of cognition?"

While Continental philosophy—particularly phenomenology—has been investigating and rendering some useful answers to these questions, anthropology has, all along, not only been raising the very same questions (albeit in many cases through indirection), but has also served as a global laboratory[6] in which these types of inquiries have been tested.

That anthropology has always been engaged in a global study of sorts of the relation between mind and culture is virtually indisputable. In many ways, Tylor (1871) initiated the anthropological inquiry into this relation when he sought to explain the origins of religion. According to Tylor, religion had its beginnings in animism, the belief in spirit beings. Animism served the psychological need of humankind to provide a causal explanation for that which was inexplicable by more rational means: aberrant states of consciousness. Thus, dreams, hallucinations, and other altered states of consciousness were explained by the presence of spirit beings. Dreams, for instance, were the results of souls—which were considered to be the second half of a soul-body duality—temporarily departing from bodies. Although Tylor was not at all interested in advancing a universal theory of consciousness, several themes, or rather tacit arguments, in his analysis of animism would continue to be revisited in the anthropological literature: that explanation and the conferral of meaning upon experience constitute psychic needs for human beings; that humans are predisposed to arranging particles of meaning into taxonomic (e.g., a tree is a variety of plant) and componential (e.g., soul and body are component parts of the human creature) systems; that the human mind functions by way of logical connection (e.g., the body has a soul, which is non-tangible and ephemeral; humans have dreams, which are non-tangible and ephemeral; therefore, it is reasonable to believe that dreaming involves the itinerant activity of the soul); that humans' psychical activity (e.g., theorizing the dyadic structure of the human individual, logical reasoning, and hierarchical arrangements of meaning) is susceptible to error;[7] and finally, that cultural forms—whether religious, juridical, or social—to some degree determined and are determined by these psychical dispositions. These themes would continue to be reworked in the likes of Fazer, Van Gennep, Levy-Bruhl, Durkheim, Malinowski, Evans-Pritchard, Radcliffe-Brown, Levi-Strauss, Douglass, Turner, and Geertz. In many ways, the functionalist, structuralist, symbolic, hermeneutic, psychological, cognitive, phenomenological, and existentialist varieties of anthropological discourse could not exist without this central preoccupation with the reciprocal relation between human consciousness and culture. It might also be argued that cultural relativism as an organizing theoretical and methodological principle would not have even emerged without this preoccupation.

Prior to this point, I have noted particular difficulties with distilling an anthropological theory of consciousness from the discipline's various theorizings about culture. The inseverability of consciousness and culture presents itself as even more intransigent when we consider anthropological analyses of an explicitly psychological nature. Consider Geertz, who set out to advance a theory of culture that was fundamentally semiotic and psychologistic. His persistence in this project is evinced in the litany of aphorisms that bedeck this magnum opus *The Interpretation of Cultures*. In the incipient essay of this collection, he states, for example, "Culture is public because meaning is" (12). Even more telling, however, is his pronouncement in the essay "Person, Time, and Conduct in Bali," in the first section, illustratively titled "The Social Nature of Thought": "Human thought is consummately social: social in its origins, social in its functions, social in its forms, social in its applications" (360).[8] The effect of such pronouncements is that they suture, irrevocably, cognition to cultural life. We see this same suturing in the phenomenological literature as well.

Let us consider Charles Laughlin and C. Jason Throop's essay, "Husserlian Meditations and Anthropological Reflections: Toward a Cultural Neurophenomenology of Experience and Reality" (2009). The authors offer that the human psyche is impressed, a priori, with certain basic existential structures operative within the "gap" between "experience and extra-mental reality." In this formulation, we see the near achievement of an anthropological theory of consciousness. However, later in the essay, the authors revisit these structures, explaining how both their existence and development are essentially cultural. The remainder of the essay, rather than advancing a theory of consciousness, advances a theory of culture, which the authors define as "a system of information." Both in framing culture as fundamentally semiotic and psychological and in subjugating the psychological in the service of the more eminent objective of defining culture, Laughlin and Throop adhere to the disciplinary precedent established by Geertz and many others.

The likes of Geertz, Durkheim, and Laughlin and Throop, and even Csordas[9] use cognition to offer a more complete understanding of culture. What I am proposing is that we perform the inverse procedure: deploy the wealth of anthropological insights regarding culture to illuminate human cognition, and by extension, human consciousness. Stated another way, rather than putting cognition in the service of culture, I would like to put culture in the service of cognition. In order to do this, we must continue to distill and elaborate upon anthropological insights regarding human cognition. At this point, however, it will not be enough to continue to simply identify themes and their textual reverberations, but rather to attend to the most urgent objective of this chapter: to name and explicate the mechanisms of cognition. In my mining of the anthropological literature, I have discovered four fundamental mechanisms of cognitive activity: *symbolization, systematization, unconscious semiosis,* and *resonation.* The first of these acknowledges that cognition involves the accretion of meanings. The second regards the fact that these accretions of meaning arrange themselves into systems of varying complexity. Unconscious semiosis indicates that accretions of meaning and systems of accretion reside in the terrain of pre-objective (unconscious) and objective (conscious) conceptualization, with infinite gradations in between. Finally, resonation references the power of symbolic configurations to effect transformations in the psychical, emotional and physiological universes of humans—in other words, the power of symbols to powerfully resonate throughout our entire beings.

Symbolization

Geertz, the Turners, and Durkheim are among those anthropologists who have established that cognition is inherently symbolic. Let us first consider Geertz's formulation of the symbolic. Because Geertz, like most sociocultural anthropologists, was primarily concerned with defining and explaining the mechanisms of culture, his assumptions regarding the components of culture assumed its attributes. Chief among these components are thought and symbols. As stated earlier, for Geertz, "[h]uman thought is consummately social." In that same essay in *The Interpretation of Cultures*, "Person, Time, and Conduct in Bali," Geertz conducts an ethnographic analysis of Balian symbolism, arriving to the nomothetic assertion that "thought does not consist of mysterious processes located in . . . a secret grotto in the head but of a traffic in significant symbols—objects in experience (rituals and tools; graven idols and water holes; gestures, markings, images, and sounds) upon which men have impressed meaning" (362). In a quite radical move, Geertz frees thought from its archetypal habitation in the heads of women and men, and locates it within the dynamic "traffic" of objects that already bear the imprint of human thought. Let us tease this out a bit. For Geertz, symbols are particles of experience that embody the thoughts of a given society. Or, as Geertz states, symbols are "the material vehicles of thought . . . [albeit] elusive, vague, fluctuating, and convoluted" (362). In addition, these symbols are somehow the content of individual moments of cognition. One can see immediately the non sequiturial nature of this formulation. If all thought is public, how can there ever be any moment of individual cognition? This formulation's particular resistance to logical resolution reflects Geertz's, and, more generally, the anthropological establishment's, resistance to an individualized notion of culture. Because definitions of culture must retain the notion of sharedness, in Geertz's semiotic definition of culture, there is no way for thought, the very arbiter of semiosis, to occur as an individual act.

One would, indeed, be justified in pointing out the absurdity of this formulation. Yet, I am convinced that the absurdity only exists at the level of rhetoric and not within the overarching spirit of Geertz's work. Surely, Geertz knows that individuals do think, and that the act of cognition itself does not require any active moments of sharing in order to be accomplished. Yet, Geertz was not interested, at least centrally, in the phenomenological content of thinking. He was only interested in putting "thinking" in the service of defining and explicating "culture." Thus, he emphasized the public aspects of thought and symbolicity.

Just as we see the individual flicker in and out of rhetorical existence in Geertz's discussion of "thought" and "symbol," said individual continues to flicker when Geertz discusses the creation of symbols. He states that

> meaning is not intrinsic in the objects, acts, processes, and so on, which bear it, but—as Durkheim, Weber, and so many others have emphasized—imposed upon them; and the explanation of its properties must therefore be sought in that which does the imposing—men living in society. (405)

Two important points emerge from this description. First, the unattended, agentive individual emerges only momentarily before s/he is quickly subsumed within the larger agency of "society." Second, and more germane to the goal of the present inquiry, symbols—avatars of meaning that they are—are constituted by intentional, arbitrary [10] acts of cognition, whereby meaning is impressed upon material and non-material entities.

Thus, if we elevate to the level of axiom Geertz's muted, subsumed premises concerning human thought, we may conclude that cognition is a fundamentally symbolic activity. We may further conclude that this activity involves two interrelated processes: (1) creation: humans create symbols by impressing meaning upon objects, both tangible (e.g., a carving, a billboard or a legal document) and intangible (a definition, a ritual, a gesture); and (2) use: humans use symbols to think—stated differently, symbols are the very substance of cognition.

If Geertz established that cognition consolidates meanings and objects into symbols, Victor Turner extended this idea to show that this consolidative process is hyper-accretive. That is, symbols absorb many meanings at once, and by extension, cognition constitutes these symbols by attaching multiple meanings to discrete cultural objects. Just as Geertz arrived at his conclusions through field studies in Bali, so Turner's insights are the result of his ethnographic study of Ndembu ritual processes in Central Africa (1985). As in Geertz's analysis, Turner's proto-theory of cognition resides in the undercurrent. Quoting Turner (1973) at length will illustrate these points:

> Thus symbol is distinguished from sign both by the multiplicity (multivocality, polysemy) of its signifieds, and by the nature of its signification. In symbols there is always some kind of likeness (metaphoric/metonymic) posited by the framing culture between signifier (symbol-vehicle) and signified(s); in signs there need be no likeness. Signs are almost always organized in "closed" systems, whereas symbols, particularly dominant symbols (which preside over

or anchor entire ritual processes), are semantically "open." The meaning is not absolutely fixed, nor is it necessarily the same for everyone who agrees that a particular signifier ("outward form") has symbolic meaning. New signifieds can be added by collective fiat to old signifiers. Moreover, individuals may add personal meanings to a symbol's public meaning, either by utilizing one of its standardized modes of association to bring new concepts within its semantic orbit (metaphorical reconstruction) or by including it within a complex of initially private fantasies. (170)

In Turner, one encounters the same difficulty present in Geertz: namely, the unsteady oscillation between the individual and the group. The question is one of residence: where do symbols and signs reside? Are they the constituents of a Kroeberian superorganic culture, or do they live in the hearts and minds of men and women? Again, I am not interested in resolving these sorts of antinomies, but rather in excavating the underlying assumptions regarding the mechanisms of cognition. With respect to this latter aim, two features are noteworthy about the foregoing quote. First, we see the same process of suturing of meanings that we encounter in Geertz—there is the more rigid, dichotomous suturing present in the constitution of signs and the more polyvalent suturing that occurs in the constitution of symbols. Second, we see the individual flicker briefly, demonstrating her/his capacity and propensity to manipulate the configuration of symbols. It should also be noted that, as in Geertz, in Turner this act of manipulation is arbitrary, or as Turner indicates, by "fiat."

Thus, we see that what I have referred to as the symbolicity of cognition may best be understood as semantic accretiveness. The simplest types of accretions are signs, which Turner considers dyadic combinations of meaning. Symbols are more complex, having infinite possibilities for the types of accretions that can occur. Metaphor, metonymy, synecdoche, analogy, and hyperbole are among the many varieties of symbolic accretion.

Predictably, therefore, both Geertz and Turner take as one of the goals of ethnographic analysis to explicate the symbolic structures of meaning with which members of societies think and interact. Both acknowledge that this task is no easy task. Geertz, for instance, understood that the elusive nature of cultural meaning makes semiotic/symbolic analysis particularly difficult for the anthropologist invested in such an enterprise. For if symbols are inherently polysemous, and exist somewhere between the ephemeral, amorphous zones of social experience and consciousness, then offering concrete, coherent, definitive explanations of symbolic systems seems virtually impossible. He warns, however, that the inherent challenges of this type of analysis should not lead one to succumb to either sterile descriptivism on one end or rigor-less impressionism on the other. The anthropologist must simply commit to the messiness of symbolic analysis. Geertz proposes as one solution to examine the objects (both empirically ascertainable and intangible) upon which humans have impressed meaning. Doing so would make "the study of culture a positive science like any other." He maintains that, despite the intractability of symbols, "they are, in principle, as capable of being discovered through systematic empirical investigation—especially if the people who perceive them will cooperate a little—as the atomic weight of hydrogen or the function of the adrenal glands" (362–363).

Turner, as is true of other phenomenologists, was more skeptical of the positivist aspirations of anthropology. His objections fit squarely within the textbook critique of positivism: that the study of culture cannot ever be predictive, that it cannot be reified as a "thing" or object, that natural laws are inapplicable to cultural artifacts, and so on. Turner's resolution to the implications of a positivist science of culture was to take, what would later come to be one of his most notable contributions to the discipline, a processual approach to cultural analysis. That is, one must consider sociality as systems of interrelated processes. Thus, anthropological analysis must be inherently processual. A hallmark of this type of analysis was the dereification of symbols and collective representations. Instead, these *nouned* entities would be *verbed*. Rather than objects, as stated in *On the Edge of the Bush*, they would be taken as "purposive and cross-purposive actions of persons in sequences of negotiations to maintain or retain, modify, or subvert social meanings, even, in some cases, to change the character and structure of common sense" (154–155).

Despite their divergent sensibilities concerning nomenclature and emphasis, upon closer examination, Geertz and Turner do not appear to be at odds methodologically. For both acknowledge that symbols are dynamic, and susceptible to alteration by human agency. Moreover, both are in agreement that the study of culture and symbols must be carried out with the utmost apperception and rigor. As Edith Turner reminds us in her introduction to *On the Edge of the Bush*, "Prologue: From the Ndembu to Broadway," Victor Turner was trained in the rigors of Max Gluckman's brand of social anthropology and "[h]e would return constantly to the grassroots, that is, to the use detailed field material to give strength to his progress" (9).

Yet, a problem continues to loom—one that lingers from the discussion of Russell: Is it possible to have a rigorous, anthropological science of consciousness? How is it possible for one to confirm that meanings, diaphanous creatures that they are, are agglomerated in particular ways? The matter of rigor becomes even more tenuous when we consider that these accretions resist delineable boundaries of time and space. The only way that such rigor can be achieved is by consulting the model put forth by analytical philosophy and mathematics. These domains of knowledge achieved their legitimacy by replacing intuition with systematicity, and doing so through an act of sheer arbitration. I propose that, through fiat, we simply reclaim the intuitive and have it exist in a dialectical synthesis with systematicity. The result would be a rigor that accepts the inevitability of intuition. Such a procedure is not unknown to anthropology. Let us recall Victor Turner's methodological declaration in *Dramas, Fields, and Metaphors: Symbolic Action in Human Society* (1974):

> The symbol, particularly the nuclear symbol, and also the plot of a ritual, had somehow to be grasped in their specific essences. In other words, the central approach to the problem of ritual has to be intuitive, although the initial intuition may then be developed in a logical series of concepts. . . . *Chihamba* is the local expression of a universal human problem, that of expressing what cannot be thought of, in view of thought's subjugation to essences. (186–187)

We see in this concise statement the reunification of the positivist emphasis on logic (although Turner adamantly eschewed the positivist project) and positivism's disavowed bastard, intuition. In addition, although Laughlin and Throop do not make any explicitly methodological statements in the aforementioned essay, they argue on many occasions in the text that intuition plays a central role in the way that meanings are combined, disseminated, and apprehended in cultural cosmologies globally. Within the logic of their own treatise, which takes great pains to equilibrate all cultural cosmologies, anthropological analysis would qualify as one such cosmology. Thus, by reasoned extension, the claims that anthropologists make regarding other peoples would have to also begin from a place of intuition.

In summary, if we synthesize the observations of Geertz, Turner, and Laughlin and Throop, then a theory of cognitive symbolization consists of the following theoretical and methodological axioms: (1) human cognition is fundamentally symbolic in nature; (2) symbols are capacious and accretive; (3) symbols have no innate properties of their own, but are the result of arbitrary acts of semantic welding; (4) symbols are dynamic and malleable; (5) therefore, the anthropologist must commit to the inherent ambiguity and complexity of such a study; (6) because symbols are dynamic, they must be studied processually; (7) the legitimacy of one's assertions regarding symbols must inevitably begin with an intuitive sense about the connections that inhere between particles of meaning; and finally, (8) the study of cognitive symbolization involves a rigorous, systematic interpretation of the analyst's intuitions.

Systemization

The systematicity of cognitive configurations is intimately connected to their symbolicity. For symbolization involves the processes by which meanings are yoked together in semi-static and utterly dynamic arrangements. The systemization of cognition refers to the particular ordering of these symbols into systems. If we use a quite imperfect metaphor from coordinate geometry, one may think of symbols as ordered pairs or points in a coordinate plane. Systems would be the arrangement of these points into patterned arrangements, or even perhaps the sets of equations that define the patterns.[11]

Both cognitive and symbolic anthropologists have been particularly instructive regarding this point. In "Toward a Convergence of Cognitive and Symbolic Anthropology" (1981), Colby, Fernandez, and Kronenfeld offer a quite useful synopsis of the development of the fields of cognitive and symbolic anthropology, critiques of both and possibilities for productive collaborations between the two. According to the authors, cognitive anthropology had historically been concerned with the logical structures that govern individuals' social realities. These structures were evident in, and could therefore be apprehended through an analysis of language. Inspired by Chomskian and Bloomfieldian linguistics, and scientific positivism, many of these anthropologists aimed to develop research designs that were hypothesis-driven, repeatable and predictive. Despite the obvious charges of reductionism and "vulgar positivism," these anthropologists of cognition generated quite impressive evidence that human cognition was predisposed to various modes of systemization. Some familiar examples of these modes are partonomic relations (part-to-whole), taxonomic (hierarchical classifications), componential (larger entities consisting of smaller components), and causal (cause-and-effect). The authors' critique of the cognitivist school is that, in reducing cultural analysis to the logical structures of thought, the experiential context of culture is lost. Whereas the cognitivists were preoccupied with isolating systems of thought from their defining contexts, symbolic anthropologists have been more concerned with understanding the constitution of symbols as functional constituents of behavioral environments. The authors' critique of the symbolic school is that, historically, it has not pursued its inquiries with the same degree of scientific rigor as has its cognitive counterpart. An ideal synthesis of the two subfields would involve a rigorous schematization of the semantic structures of cognition, and an equally rigorous analysis of the reciprocal relation between those structures and the cultural field. Ohnuki-Tierny (1981), Sapir (1981), and Parker (1988) all provide excellent examples of the type of synthesis that Colby, Fernandez, and Kronenfeld advise.

Unconscious Semiosis

Traditionally, the unconscious has been most abundantly theorized within the field of psychoanalysis. And certainly, many disciplines, not just anthropology, have benefited from psychoanalytic insights. Yet, in its vast, multicultural, multi-sited laboratory, anthropology has generated some truly pioneering observations regarding the unconscious. Chief among these observations is the understanding that symbols and systems of symbolic meaning are assembled unconsciously.

In "Hypocognition, a 'Sense of the Uncanny,' and the Anthropology of Ambiguity: Reflections on Robert I. Levy's Contribution to Theories of Experience in Anthropology" (2005), Throop demonstrates how Levy's monograph *Tahitians* (1973) prefigures the phenomenological study of the two modalities of consciousness: the pre-objective and the objective. For Throop, the two modes run along a continuum from the pre-objective—activities of consciousness that elude explicit awareness (hypocognition)—to the objective—the overt constitution and traffic of meanings. We see in Throop the implicit argument that human cognition is predisposed to organizing meaning into coordinate points and patterned systems. Yet Throop adds to this conception that the degree to which meanings are integrated varies—some meanings are integrated seamlessly, while others are integrated with various degrees of incongruity. Complicating this picture even further is the pre-objective/objective continuum of cognition. The influence of a network of symbols depends upon the intentional focus of the individual. While some symbolic configurations are actively engaged and contemplated at various moments of social experience, others remain at the fringes of awareness. Whether at the center or the periphery of awareness, those meaning clusters that have an incongruous, uncategorizable relation to more systematized networks of meaning tend to constitute what Throop calls the "uncanny."[12] Whereas for Throop, the unconscious is a site for both assimilated and unintegrated cultural material, for Hollan, the unconscious is the exclusive territory of the inevitably copious data that remain unincorporated and uncodified in the incessant flow of social engagements (2000). Whether there is more merit to Hollan's or Throop's position will have to be resolved upon further field studies. At present, it is enough to recognize their concurrence that the unconscious is a site of semiosis.

That culturally derived meanings dwell beneath the surface of conscious awareness has been variously indicated throughout the trajectory of anthropological musings. Stocking recounts Boas's observation, for instance, that our beliefs and behaviors are unconscious genuflections to "the general conditions of life" (1968). Levi-Strauss (1978), Bourdieu (1977), Sapir (1981), Csordas (1990, 1994), and Crapanzano (2004) also observe that much of the culturally determined material of cognition eludes conscious awareness. Many of these thinkers, particularly Levi-Strauss, Bourdieu, Hollan, Throop, and Crapanzano, and many others in the cognitivist and symbolist schools, suggest that it is the hiddenness of this material that makes it that much more compelling of human thought and behavior.

Accessing the symbolic content of the unconscious has unique challenges for the anthropologist. Cognitive anthropologists have known for quite some time that a thorough understanding of cognition requires one to penetrate the deep structure of the unconscious. Because they assume that there is an intimate correlation between the rules of language, which largely elude conscious awareness, and the mechanisms governing cognition, they also hold that these mechanisms must be treated in part as unconscious entities. As such, the analyst must get at this unconscious material through various methods of indirection (Foster 1973).

In sociocultural anthropology more generally, it has been common practice that any consideration of the unconscious or any other concept having its origins in psychoanalysis has evoked the insights of the latter field. For instance, Hollan, who is both a psychological anthropologist and practicing psychoanalyst, advocates a synthesis between cultural phenomenology and psychoanalysis, a synthesis that he has utilized in his own work (2012). Weiss and Stanek found it useful in their study of the *naven* ritual in Papua New Guinea to collaborate with a team of psychoanalysts, using the latter's clinical methods during ethnographic interviews (2007). As a final example, in what could be classified as a symbolic analysis of the Yagwoian unconscious, Mimica deploys Freudian psychoanalytic concepts that are "phenomenologically grounded in the Yagwoia life-world" (2007).[13] As the aforementioned authors demonstrate, anthropological exploration of the unconscious could benefit tremendously from a synthesis of methods deriving from cognitive and symbolic anthropology, and psychoanalysis.

Resonation

As part of the defining content of our objective and pre-objective awareness, symbolic meaning, as implied or explicitly argued by several anthropologists, is profoundly resonant—that is, symbols beget experience, compel behavior, incite emotion, and ultimately, beget other symbols. Returning to Durkheim, in *Elementary Forms*, the author notes that symbols are not just evocative of powerful emotions, but that they are instrumental in eliciting actual transformations in the constitution mind and body (Olaveson 2001). In his famous analysis of fetish objects, Durkheim argues that the accretion of meaning represented by the fetish object creates the sense that that object is somehow "charged" with a spiritual essence. Such entities—whether material or purely semantic—have a powerful influence over thought and behavior. Geertz corroborates the idea that symbols are potent transformers of reality: "For human beings . . . all experience is construed experience and the symbolic forms in terms of which it is construed thus determine. . . . its intrinsic structure" (*The Interpretation of Cultures*, 405). Jackson admits a similar point: that metaphors are the non-dualistic content of experience itself (1989).

That the symbolic content of the mind could not only motivate thought and behavior, but could transform the total consciousness and being of the individual is observed most poignantly in Edith Turner's 1992 *Experiencing Ritual*. Much of the text involves the author's coming to terms with seeing a spirit in an Ndembu ritual context. Turner's encounter with the spirit being occurred at a crescendo in the ritual process. She explains that at the moment of the sighting, not only had the ritual fervor in the room reached a peak, but all who were present, including Turner herself, were somewhat desperate for the ceremony to prove itself efficacious. It was the convergence of all these elements that led to the eventual witnessing of the black spirit ether that had already been codified within the Ndembu culture. This experience led her to some important conclusions regarding the relation between symbols and phenomenological experience. In alignment with her husband, Edith Turner concluded that symbols serve as pathways to other realms of being. Evoking Levi-Strauss and Levi-Bruhl, she argues that, because symbols are convergent zones between domains of meaning, they can actually effect changes in the physical and mental constitution of individuals.

Desjarlais makes a similar point in his analysis of shamanism in Nepal (1989). He demonstrates how the shamanic journey is simultaneously a traversal of the myth-laden local geography and of the symbolic structures that have been culturally affixed to that geography. The spiritual journey to a particular place in the Nepalese landscape parallels, and thereby institutes, the patient's journey from a condition of dis-ease to one of wellness. The metaphorical journey has physiologically efficacious consequences.

What Edith Turner, Desjarlais, Durkheim, Jackson, and others offer, therefore, is a symbolicist explanation for psychoanalytic and psychosomatic processes.

Summary

In this section I have argued that symbols, constituted and circulated in the cauldron of cultural experience, comprise a significant portion of the content of cognition. Symbols, however, predictably participating in the attributes of cognition itself, are by no means static. Instead, they are dynamic, accretive and recombinant; they range in capaciousness from dyadic units to polyvalent clusters, and arrange themselves into systems. There are even particles of meaning that have not been codified as symbols per se (for symbol, by definition, must consist of at least two parts), but exist as idiosyncratic free radicals of sorts. Furthermore, cognition is both objective and pre-objective, residing simultaneously in the content of our intentional foci and interactions, and in the penumbral chambers of the unconscious. Finally, symbols, the very content of cognition, are motivating, compelling, even transforming of corporeal, perceptual, cognitive, and emotional realities.

The unwieldy dynamism of symbolic forms necessitates a methodology that strategically combines principles derived from ethnographic praxis, symbolic anthropology (which includes anthropology of ritual and anthropology of religion), cognitive anthropology, and psychoanalysis. Informed by these principles, an analysis of the symbolic content of cognition would involve (1) meticulously gathering fieldwork data; (2) distilling and sorting the symbolic/semantic content of the data; (3) drawing parallels between the cultural context and symbolic material; and (4) utilizing psychoanalytic methods to access unconscious symbolic content.

AN ANTHROPOLOGICAL THEORY OF EMOTION

In many ways, the study of emotion has brought about even more difficulties than the study of cognition. While both emotion (also referred to as affect or feeling) shares with cognition the quality of empirical inaccessibility, the latter, at least in the public imaginary, is more amenable to the discourses of common sense, logic, and reasoning. Neurophysiological and evolutionary considerations aside (as these are beyond the scope of the current exposition), the emotions constitute an ontological crisis for philosophers and social scientists alike, both of whom are hard pressed to explain their composition, origin and consequences. Anthropologists, who historically have restricted themselves to the observation of social phenomena, have dealt with affect in a variety of ways, ranging from outright avoidance to imperiled (intellectually) forays into uncovering its exact ontology.

In the introductory chapter to *In the Midst of Life: Affect and Ideation in the World of the Tolai*, Epstein offers a cogent analysis of some of the ways anthropologists have handled the problem of affect (1992). According to Epstein, early anthropologists tended to avoid affect altogether, as it is too slippery to be instructive for a science that is highly dependent on the observation of sociological facts. Epstein cites Knapp's summary of the seemingly insurmountable challenges to studying affect thus: "like a mountain peak, emotional experience has an apparent immediacy and concreteness, yet a way of receding into a conceptual haze" (2). Rather than concern themselves with data that are inherently volatile and impermanent, anthropologists chose to confine their inquiries to features of human societies that could be subjected to various tests of validity and verifiability. Not everyone was intimidated by the difficulties posed by intractable data, however. Because the express aim of ethnographic study has always been to elucidate the system of meaning of the other, many anthropologists understood how an understanding of their subjects' emotions was indispensable to anthropological analysis. Much of this early work on affect focused on deciphering other cultures' linguistic registers for describing emotional states. Predictably, this work evoked some of the linguistic/semantic methods indicated earlier. To illustrate this point, Epstein references his own particular challenges to translating these registers in various ethnographic contexts from one language to another. With the problem of translation naturally came that of universality.

If emotion terms could be translated between languages, then certain emotional constructs are universal, and are thus not at all culturally determined. If terms are not translatable, then the implication would be that emotions are completely dictated by culture. At present, the consensus is that universal patterns of affect do exist, even as culture plays a large role in determining both the content and expression of emotion (Postert 2012, Simon 2005).

Since the early anthropological treatments of affect—which tended to range from dismissal to description—the field has become much more sophisticated, producing insights relevant for both the ontology and the cultural functionality of the emotions. Anthropologists have variously asked the bold, intimidating questions that have harassed scholars across the disciplines: What are the emotions? What incites particular emotions? What function do they serve for the individual and the society? In asking these very questions of their field data, which have now spanned three centuries and myriad locations across the globe, anthropologists have illumined a field of study that at one time appeared to be profoundly opaque and impervious to rigorous social scientific study. I will concentrate on two fundamental insights that may be distilled from the anthropological record: (1) that emotions appear to be the epiphenomenal residue of particular existential conditions; and (2) that emotion is a manner of comporting oneself to a specific cultural context. I indicate each phenomenon as *epiphenomenality* and *comportmentality*, respectively.

Epiphenomenality

The word "epiphenomenal" has become somewhat anathema in the anthropology of consciousness, and in particular, phenomenological anthropology. The reason is that the term implies a sense of the consequent, which further suggests a preeminence of one mode of consciousness or existential being over another. For example, one would never commit the heresy of proposing that consciousness is epiphenomenal to neurotransmission. We anthropologists would like to think (and for good reason) that cognition, emotion, and the intricate circuitry of the central nervous system work in simultaneity. I agree wholeheartedly. Despite mine and other anthropologists' convictions regarding this issue, however, in my own reading of anthropological studies of affect, I am inclined to argue that even our most astute anthropologists have discovered—although they have not acknowledged the fact as a moment of explicit theorizing—epiphenomenality describes one type of relation between emotion and other modes of consciousness. Stated another way, some anthropologists have uncovered that emotions emerge as a type of residue, a reflection of particular circumstances.

Evoking William Reddy (2001), Cati Coe offers an analysis of the emotional suffering experienced by Ghanaian parents and children as a result of either's migration to other countries (2008). Reddy argues that emotions are "closely associated with the dense networks of goals that give coherence to the self," and they "aid the individual in managing the conflicting tugs and contradictions that the pursuit of multiple goals must give rise to" (Reddy 2001: 55). For Reddy, "emotional suffering arises from the conflict between high-priority, culturally-significant goals, as when one wishes to be close to someone who does not love one or when one is being tortured during interrogation and wishes to preserve both one's health and dignity" (Coe 2008: 223). Coe revises Reddy's framework, arguing that a given emotion (e.g., sadness) is not the inevitable result of particular circumstances (e.g., separation from loved ones). Factors such as social position and prior values contribute to emotional experiences. For instance, the normative discourse of home and nuclear family consists of parents living at home with all of their children in one place, with the mother providing both emotional and material support. Within the logic of this scenario, the notions of home and nurturance may be expanded, such that the parent is away and still providing material support, and the child receives emotional support from a grandparent. Thus, during the absence of parents, a child may or may not long for them or the nuclear family, all depending on whether or not the requirements for emotional connection and material support are met. Thus, we see that the very content of emotion is largely determined by culture and circumstance.

We witness the same epiphenomenality of emotion with Desjarlais as well (1994). In his study of a Boston homeless shelter, he noticed that how the Western philosophical tradition defines "experience" itself was not applicable to the indigents that resided at the shelter. Experience in a Western sense involves a sense that the events in one's life are connected thematically and temporally. Yet, Desjarlais's research subjects, who in many regards represent all who live on the fringes of post-industrial American society, lived in a way that was directly antithetical to this portrait. They did not seem to experience, but rather "struggle along." What is remarkable about the essay itself is that Desjarlais shows the progression of research subjects, from their initial admittance to the shelter to their full integration—their matriculation from the domain of experience to that of simply struggling along. Aside from the astuteness of his interrogation of the ontology of experience itself, Desjarlais demonstrates how particular emotional states were the direct, complex manifestations of very particular cultural circumstances.

As the reflective emanations of sociocultural predicaments, emotions have also been cast as the more viscerally felt element of a cognitive arrangement. In this formulation, cognition and emotion are continuous and indissociable.[14] Goluboff (2011) makes this point cogently in her study of African Americans' emotional attachment to their "homeplace," a conceptual synthesis of their geographical place of origin, their family, and their church. Invoking Nussbaum, Goluboff shows, for instance, that emotional attachment is an embodied judgment of value. For the members of the African American community under investigation, the fondness for homeplace was the viscerally felt judgment of the value that they had already ascribed to that homeplace.

As Reddy, Coe, Desjarlais, and Goluboff demonstrate, a serious consideration of emotions absolutely requires that the researcher understand the cultural context in which these emotions manifest, and investigate precisely how they reflect that context.

Comportmentality

While the examples presented above represent the epiphenomenalism of anthropological studies of affect, those presented here move in the opposite direction, showing that the emotions have been studied as a manner (and in some cases, even a strategy) for existing within one's circumstances.

Illustrative of this point, Ramos-Zayas (2011) conducted an ethnographic study of Latina(o) youth who had emigrated from various parts of Latin America to Newark, New Jersey. One part of her study deals with what she calls the "emotional labor" in which these individuals engaged in order to adjust to their new cultural landscape. Ramos-Zayas demonstrates that in order for these Latin American immigrants to properly integrate into the predominantly black urban setting of Newark, they had to "learn" how to be "depressed," thereby reflecting the dominantly prescribed mood of Newark African Americans and achieving a type of racialized affective "legibility." In her subtle investigations of the ontology of what she calls "negative affect," Ramos-Zayas shows that the immigrant community actively participated in a type of education, whereby they would learn to "be hard" and "depressed," and teach themselves how to forsake the "cheerfulness" and "naivete" commonly associated with unassimilated Latina(o)s. In this way, affect is not simply the emergent property of particular circumstances as seen earlier, but rather an actively cultivated comportment for living within those circumstances.

Postert (2012) shows the co-occurrence of epiphenomenality and comportmentality in Hmong gift and commodity exchanges. Within the complex systems of reciprocal exchange among the Hmong, as is generally true in most societies dependent on systems of exchange, there always arises the possibility for unevenness, or parties feeling as if they have not gotten their proper share. When this scenario occurs or at least the threat of it is imminent, then that particular party may fall into *tu siab*, roughly translated as "depressed mood." While tu siab is a reaction to the threat of distributional unevenness, it also provides a means of regulating the proper order of reciprocal exchanges. In short, Postert argues that tu siab is a "bidirectional" process that both reflects and functionally maintains the social order.

Consistent with the work of Postert and Ramos-Zayas, Hollan's study of the Toraja in Indonesia shows how affect is not simply reflective, but is rather agentively allowed and constructed (2008). Hollan, drawing upon the insights of Halpern, understands empathy to be not some moment of spiritual exchange between subjects, but rather an imaginative act, by which the empathizer cognizes a relation between herself/himself and another. Thus, empathy is cognitive and emotional simultaneously. Hollan urges further, however, that we must not devote all of our attention to the ways in which the empathizer comes to relate to his/her object, but also direct our focus to how the recipients of empathetic sentiments allow themselves to be empathically legible. This point emerged from Hollan's interactions with his field-subjects, as he noticed that the degree to which he could understand or empathize with them was to a large degree determined by how well they wanted to be understood. Hollan shows us that affect may not only involve the manner in which subjects position themselves with respect to one another, but also how the investigators position themselves with relation to their subjects, and how their subjects allow themselves to be positioned with respect to their investigators

Summary

I prefer to think of epiphenomenal and comportmental attributes of emotion as complementary rather than existing in some sort of potentially unresolvable tension. I see no problem with understanding them to be simultaneously the intuitively felt emanations of particular cultural realities and modes of visceral modification with which people situate themselves inside of these very circumstances. With respect to the former, Nussbaum and Goluboff argue that there is no separation between cognition and affect, but rather that they are part of a phenomenological continuum. Others admit the intimately intertwined nature of the two, although these scholars do not necessarily conceive of them as continuous. Moreover, emotion, as Postert shows, may be socially and culturally regulative. In the study of affect, three principles must maintain: (1) harking back to Epstein's admonition, one must be vigilant to delineate the emotional cosmology of research subjects, paying attention to gradations of meaning and how terms are consonant and dissonant with those of the ethnographer's language; (2) the researcher must also detail the sociocultural matrix in which the emotional field is integrated, establishing, where applicable, correlations between the two; and finally (3) one must understand the emotional phenomenology of the research subjects to be at once epiphenomenal and comportmental.

In our present search for the mechanisms of consciousness, namely cognition and emotion, many new difficulties have inevitably arisen, particularly regarding the consciousness of individuals. One might ask: What are the mechanisms by which meanings accrete to form symbols? What are the mechanisms by which the individual internalizes symbolic fields? What is the procedure by which symbolic networks activate the semi-autonomous register known as the pre-objective? How do people cultivate particular emotion repertoires, particularly those that are enduring? Where is the nexus between cognition and emotion? To answer these and related questions, I turn now to Sartre for his insights concerning individual consciousness and to the Africana existentialist tradition to illuminate the intersubjective play of consciousnesses.

SARTRE'S EXISTENTIAL PSYCHOANALYSIS: FUNDAMENTAL PROJECTION, LIVING, AND TROPOLOGICAL DENSITIES

In *Being and Nothingness* (1993), Jean-Paul Sartre proposed that human beings are essentially "free." Sartrean freedom is not that found in colloquial or juridical usages, however. Sartre only means to indicate that great, expansive infinitude that he calls "consciousness," or in his own lexicon, the "for-itself." If we appeal to our basic common sense about things, Sartre's precept is certainly within our grasp; we can conceive of the mind's ability to traverse many dimensions, high and low, unbound by the physical laws of our cosmos. And, the commonsense approach to the for-itself is not inconsistent with, what I believe to be, Sartre's own sense of that interminable vista. However, when Sartre evokes the notion of "freedom," he is more centrally concerned with the capacity of the self to "choose" who it is—its "being." In fact, Sartre maintained that the defining mark of the human being is that it does not have the option of not choosing how the for-itself is configured. Every conscious being must define himself or herself through a choice.

And yet, this allegory of the "everyman" is complicated by Sartre's well-reasoned intuition that consciousness is always in the process of deceiving itself into believing that it has made no choice at all. Said everyman, according to Sartre, has deceived himself into thinking that he is a fixed entity—a singer, for instance. What remains hidden is the fact that one can choose at any given moment to abandon that vocation, and become an architect, or even a serial killer. Thus, the imagined fixity of that one's position in the world is nothing more than the effect of a more fundamental choice to inhabit that position at every moment. The iterative genesis of that choice, and what Sartre claims to be the anxiety of not occupying any position at all (which is never a possibility in Sartre's mythology, as consciousness always has to be consciousness of something) and the inherent, futile urge to be a fixity—or what Sartre calls the "in-itself" (also known as a "thing")—conspire to hide the fact of the initial choosing. Sartre refers to this hiding as the condition of living in "bad faith." According to Sartre, none of us is exempt from bad faith, given that the choice of who we are will never be unalterable. Consciousness can never relinquish the capacity to choose (as long as it is indeed consciousness and has not exhausted itself in comatosity or death), thereby becoming a thing. Thus, to live in "good faith," while a seeming ideal, is impossible (as it is, generally, with ideals), as this condition would preclude the inherently generative activity of consciousness. In the Sartrean matrix, to be human is to be fundamentally deluded. To ever recede from the entrapments of bad faith and orient oneself in the not so disingenuous direction of an unachievable state of good faith is all for which one could possibly hope.

From Sartre's topography of consciousness/freedom, choice, bad faith, and good faith emerges his "existential psychoanalysis." According to this theory, every person makes a fundamental choice (also called a "project") of whom he or she is. This choice functions as a motor, dictating the nature of all secondary choices and determining the color of one's experiences. Sartre contends that the for-itself is powerless to this sovereign choice, as, according to its nature, it is shrouded in bad faith. Sartre takes one step further to argue that the choice is just the result of self-deception; it is also completely inaccessible. As an existentialist analog to Mary Shelley, consciousness, which sired the choice, does not even have the resources to alter it. Sartre argues that the psychoanalyst must somehow excavate the fundamental project if that one hopes to liberate an individual from the pathologies that emerge from various degrees of bad faith. In short, Sartre desires a new form of psychoanalysis, one not based on what he considers to be the deterministic logic of Freud's drives, but rather upon the self-accountability (although albeit self-encumbering) of consciousness and the fundamental choice. With all his methodological ambitions, however, Sartre arrives to the end of *Being and Nothingness* with no explanation for how these "choices" emerge or how they might come to be altered.

Subsequent to the publication of his magnum opus, Sartre gives concrete manifestation to his theory of existential psychoanalysis by examining the lives of the French authors Baudelaire (1950) and Flaubert (1993). His meditations upon the German occupation of France during World War II are most instructive (2008) for the present discussion, however; for in these essays (particularly, "Paris under the Occupation"), Sartre applies his insights to the collective national consciousness of France at the time. Chief among his assertions is that the Occupation brought about a fundamental change in the consciousness of the French citizens. Sartre implies that, when they had previously lived in a state of juridical and situational freedom, somehow their thoughts and actions lacked authenticity. In other words, they were unwittingly conforming to the logic of bad faith. Yet, inhabiting a situational unfreedom had the opposite effect:

Because the Nazi venom seeped into our very thoughts, every accurate thought was a triumph. Because an all-powerful police force tried to gag us, every word became precious as a declaration of principle. Because we were wanted men and women, every one of our acts was a solemn commitment. The often atrocious circumstances of our struggle made it possible, in a word, for us to live out that unbearable, heart-rending situation known as the human condition in a candid, unvarnished way. (3–4)

In this analysis, bad faith becomes the desired orientation. For, prior to the Occupation, the citizens of France had the luxury of existing noncommittally. One must be careful not to assign positive or negative value to either bad or good faith, however, as they do nothing more than describe the complex, counterintuitive manner in which consciousness is configured. What is more important to note here is how the all-consuming predicament of "struggle" was able to permanently shift consciousness, propelling it in the direction of good faith. Sartre continues by suggesting that this "shift" conduced to a fundamentally different "choosing": "Each, standing against the oppressors, made the effort to be himself irremediably" (6). In sum, struggle was the catalyst for the transformation of the Parisian citizens' fundamental project. Consciousness itself, through its defining mechanism of choice, had made the project a complete life orientation.

In addition to explicating how fundamental projection is instituted, Sartre demonstrates the ways in which projection plays out in the realm of experience. He states in one place that his aim is "to try to show how the Parisians experienced the Occupation emotionally" (11). He continues: "But one should not forget that the Occupation was a daily affair. Someone who was asked what he had done under the Terror said, 'I lived. . . .' It is an answer we could all give today" (11–12). Here, the construct of "living" not only indicates that the Occupation was a "daily affair," but it more subtly intimates the nature of the fundamental choice itself. These citizens could only inhabit a space somewhere between their discontent at the Occupation and the choice that they had made to inwardly resist this predicament. Theirs was a condition of restless ennui.

Sartre continues his characterization of the Parisian experience with several phenomenological accounts, such as the one that follows:

There was not one in Paris who had not had a relative or friend arrested or sent to the camps or shot. There seemed to be hidden holes in the city and it seemed to empty itself through these holes, as though it had some undetectable internal haemorrhage. We did not talk about it much, in fact; we covered up this uninterrupted bloodletting even more than we did the hunger, partly out of caution and partly for reasons of dignity. (16)

Sartre had already established at an earlier point in the narrative that torture, suffering, and the threat of death's fulfillment (since its actual fulfillment is a negation of human experience) represent the infernal extremities of all possible human experiences. To these individual experiences is now added a different agglomeration of predicaments: that which is contingent upon sympathetic identification with others. Sartre's imaginative-tropological landscape is the enfleshment of this very existential assault, both upon self and other. Articulated another way, textual images, far from literary embellishments or non-material reflections of experience, become, for Sartre, dense materializations of experience. The "hidden holes," for instance, are simultaneously textual, imaginative and actual. They were just as much a part of the landscape of Paris as they were topographical features of the existential landscape of Parisian consciousness at that time.

Along with the experience of abduction, the threat of abduction and the experience of the abduction of another, German soldiers also achieved tropological density:

> We said, "They've arrested him" and this "they," similar to that used at times by madmen to name their fictitious persecutors, barely referred to human beings: it referred more to a kind of intangible, living tar that blackened everything, even the light. (16)

Paradoxical duality characterizes these German soldiers. They are incorporeal and diffuse, yet they are the definitive, material sources of a "blackened" experience of "everything." What must also be noted is that these soldiers flicker at the inseverable seam of "objective reality" and the subjective realm of interiority.

What Sartre's meditation upon the Parisian citizens suggests is that it is at this very seam—that region of convergence between pneuma and phenomena—that all tropes arising within experience achieve a compelling, ontological density.

In sum, dissatisfied with Freudian determinism, Sartre positioned choice at the epicenter of a revised psychological troposphere, which he appropriately named "existential psychoanalysis." At base, he wanted it to be clear that consciousness, and by extension, the activity of choosing, are inalienable features of human existence. The nature of consciousness is such that it yearns for fixity, to be a thing. In asserting its stability, however, consciousness hides from itself that it has indeed chosen to be fixed, an inexorable deception known as bad faith. Good faith, then, would be the recognition of our inherent changeability. Yet, because we must always choose to be something at every given moment, it is impossible for one to remain in a pure condition of good faith. Sartre conceives of these choices as preconscious and inaccessible. He calls them "fundamental projects" to indicate that they structure phenomenological experience in a foundational way. In *Aftermath of War*, Sartre seeks to understand how fundamental projects are formed and changed, and how they conduce to phenomenological experience. He implies that these projects are initiated by severe, all-consuming assaults on humanity, then, achieve relative fixity through the subjective machinations of choice. "Living," therefore, becomes the phenomenological nexus, in which one daily and iteratively recuperates a choice to exist within a socio-historically defined reality in particular, tropologically specific ways.

Neither in *Being and Nothingness*, his psycho-biographies, nor in *Aftermath of War*, however, does Sartre consider how phenomenological experience might be constituted at the crossroads of multiple, competing fundamental projects. The Africana existentialist tradition is particularly useful for extending Sartre's insights in these ways.

EXISTENTIA AFRICANA:
THE INTERSUBJECTIVE FORMULATION OF BLACK BEING

According to Lewis Gordon in *Existential Africana: Understanding Africana Existential Thought* (2000), the broad-scale system of racial hegemony—initiated by the Atlantic and Indian slave trade and European colonialism—defined the general predicament of Africana peoples [15] in the modern era. For not only did this era witness the intense suffering of black people, but it also marked the ascendency of the "hegemonic symbolic order of Western civilization itself " (9), establishing the inferiority of everything that was not white. It is important to note also that, unlike the situation that Sartre chronicled in France during World War II, racial hegemony has been gaining momentum for more than five hundred years, affecting all those born into its territory. Gordon further contends that, because this system of hegemony has served to, at every turn, negate the very humanity of Africana peoples, Africana thought—both within and beyond the realm of letters—has always been centrally occupied with questions of existence and humanity; in other words, Africana philosophical thought is inherently existentialist. Gordon supports his claim both in the aforementioned work and elsewhere with a remarkable catalogue of Africana thinkers that fit squarely into this tradition of Africana existentialism—figures such as Angela Davis, Martin Delaney, Ralph Ellison, Frederick Douglass, Anna Julia Cooper, Cornel West, bell hooks, Paget Henry, and Frantz Fanon, just to name a few (1998).

In existential psychoanalytic parlance, racial hegemony constitutes a diffuse socio-historical reality for both Africana and white people. The preoccupation with questions of how Africana peoples can reclaim a confiscated humanity, then, would be the beginning of their fundamental project. By contrast, the continuing of the system of Western hegemony would form the basis of the fundamental project of white subjects. The question then arises: How are the experiences of blacks and whites constituted through the intersubjective play of divergent fundamental projects? The interplay of black and white being has been the focal point of many examinations of colonial and postcolonial realities. Consequently, many Africana philosophers from geographically diverse regions have identified the notion of "racism" as the central problematic.

Manganyi, for instance, constructs an elaborate psycho-existential typology that defines the very logic and functioning of modern-day racism (1981). He argues that racism is rooted in a universal antinomy between the finitude of the body and the mind's infinite capacity for symbolization. In this formulation, the human being is apt to construct symbolizations in which he or she is the embodiment of all that is good and desirable, while an Other is constructed as the reservoir of all that stands in opposition. The most fundamental of these Manichean symbolizations relegates the body to an inferior position (because it is subject to death and decay), and assigns desirability to the mind. The schema becomes a repeating set of dichotomous signs, in which the body is associated with death, sexuality, evil, animality, and blackness, while the mind becomes metonymically attached to spirit, moral virtue, humanity, and whiteness. In the logic of white supremacy, therefore, the Africana person is, symbolically, everything that would preclude a transcendent, disembodied whiteness. Manganyi also contends, in Lacanian fashion, that the "real" is trapped within a dogged cycle of resurrection and crucifixion. In its inevitable, cyclical return, the real of embodied blackness becomes so many objects of desire, the very desire that promptly conveys this blackness to the "nether" regions for the slaughter. Regarding this latter idea, Gilroy (2000), Stuart (2005), and St. Louis (2005) have all argued that the figuration of the black body as hyperphysicality and hypersexuality accounts for the fact that the most iconic black figures tend to derive their renown from their associations with beauty, athleticism, or other modes of physicality. Predictably then, those figures who inspire the most dread and contempt are those whose symbolization has also been unfortunately yoked to these same modes. For Manganyi, humans' psycho-existential fissuring of body and mind, this division's translation into Manichean symbolizations of whiteness and blackness, and the cyclical and mutually constitutive nature of negrocidal and negrophilic fixations all account for the recalcitrance of racist ideologies.

Yancy offers similar presuppositions, yet does so through the prism of historical materialism (2004). The foundation of his project is that race, though not "natural" in the scientific sense, is nevertheless ontological, and, henceforth, compelling. Articulated in other terms, racial understandings arrive onto the scene already having achieved tropological density. The two ontological identities under investigation, "whiteness" and "blackness," for

Yancy, are locked in a relation of inseverable interdependence, and define an all-consuming totality for colonial and postcolonial subjects. In the same edited volume, Robert Birt extends this point through Sartre's formulation of "bad faith." Evoking the Sartrean typology that Thomas Martin established, Birt contends that there exist two modes of bad faith—that which is a flight from transcendence into facticity and that relation's obverse (2004). Continuous with Manganyi's dichotomous system, Birt posits that whiteness consigns blackness to the domain of facticity, flees from that execrable domain, and then sublimates itself as pure transcendence. In denying the transcendence of the "Other," he concludes, whiteness constitutes itself as a "parasitic identity" (58). Birt's analysis derives its utility from its suggestion that racist configurations emerge as a function of intersubjective play. In order for his insights to achieve their highest explicatory value, however, his appropriation of the Sartrean typology must be somewhat complicated. For Sartre, "transcendence" was not the etheric entity of Transcendentalism, but rather the inexorable persistence of choice and the latter's structure of mutability. If anything, then, whiteness flees from its own ontic chosenness, endeavoring, anachronistically, to found itself as providentially chosen—a veritable in-itself.

Yet, if we take Manganyi's insights seriously, and if we find merit in Sartre's ruminations upon the incessant and dynamic oscillations between good and bad faith (and the in-itself and the for-itself, for that matter), then it becomes clear that neither whiteness nor blackness could ever achieve true ontological closure. Whiteness must be taken as a kinetic procedure that actively recognizes itself, in good faith, as consciously chosen, only in the same moment to assume the mantle of given-ness—a given-ness that is nothing more than a synthesis of all that is transcendent in our dichotomous symbolic order. Blackness serves as the ontologically kinetic foundation and antithesis of whiteness. In its circadian fervor, the procedure for the establishment of blackness is comparable to that for whiteness. The Africana person is acknowledged as being the rightful heir of consciousness and its near infinitude of potentiality; either synchronically or diachronically, that human potential is disavowed; the Africana subject is divested of emotional sentience and reason, the critical markers of humanity (Bell 1998, Hartman 1997). Birt's own insights—gleaned partly from Sartre's analysis of the relation between "slaves" and "masters" in *Critique of Dialectical Reasoning*—attests to this latter procedure. He argues that in order for blackness to be equated with animality, for instance, there must be an initial recognition of humanity and its subsequent denial (60).

If Yancy, Birt, and Manganyi have established racism as the ontological foundation of intersubjective relationships in the post-colonial world, Gordon further helps us to understand how this foundation reverberates as an institutional reality for black people. Gordon argues that black people exist under the weight of "oppression," an analytic that he infuses with existential import. For Gordon, oppression is a condition whereby a people's life-options and capacity for self-assertion as human beings have been severely circumscribed. Cornel West corroborates this point, insisting that the institutional character of racism serves to foreclose the positive assertion of individual freedom (1982). Just as Gordon and West help us understand how lived experience is the densest manifestation of our symbolic order, Derek Hooks helps us see even more acutely how that order is experienced at the level of corporeality (2008). For Hooks, "the body" is a "living vessel" for these "ideological meanings" (143). Corporeality is the very seat through which the sensations (if they can be narrowly classified as such) of pain, suffering, and fear are experienced. Furthermore, the very processes whereby we become subjects occur through the medium of the body. In short, racist logic conditions the total ontology of Africana peoples—symbolically, institutionally, and corporeally. Two questions therefore remain: How have black people chosen to live within the condition of racism? Who have we chosen ourselves to be?

Earlier, through Gordon, I suggested that the system of racial hegemony has created a condition in which Africana peoples are centrally preoccupied with questions of humanity and being. The work of many Africana existential philosophers corroborates this position and further recommends that Africana peoples are directly invested in disfiguring the symbolic order and its manifestations as corporeal and institutional realities. Frederick Douglass's narrative, for instance, offers an incisive analysis of the contested humanity of the black slave, particularly regarding education (1846). When Mr. Auld forbade his wife Sophia from continuing to impart the skill of literacy, it became immediately apparent to Douglass just what was at stake in teaching the slave how to read. For Douglass, denying literacy to the slave was a cruel form of objectification, whereby the one in bondage was completely divested of the potential to cultivate his or her mental and moral faculties. Mr. Auld made it clear that to educate Douglass or any slave, for that matter, would have been to risk the slave even knowing that he or she should be disconsolate. The intention was to make the slave into a social non-being (West 1982). Thus, for Douglass, as both Gordon and Stephen Haymes (2001) point out, the acquisition of literacy was directly connected to the project of reclaiming a confiscated humanity. Gordon suggests, therefore, that the slave's existence was essentially teleological, always projecting itself toward a desired future of fulfilled humanity (Levine 1978, Webber 1978, Henry 2000).

To argue that the one who suffers under racial oppression is always oriented toward a telos of reclaimed humanity, however, would nullify all of Sartre's fundamental propositions, undermine his entire cosmology, and undo the very premise upon which the present exposition has been established. Let us emerge from this logical quagmire by continuing with the example of the slave. If Sartre is correct, then the position "slave" would have to be inhabited in bad faith, implying that the slave hides from the fact that he or she has freely chosen this position and has other options. And, certainly, the slave does have other options. There is the option to escape, which could result in sadistic forms of cruelty and death—of self and/or kin. There is the option of transgression, which would have the same consequences. Finally, there is the option of suicide (a significant percentage of slaves did indeed choose this non-predicament) (Snyder 2010). And, there were slaves who did, indeed, choose to be renegades, martyrs, and legal transgressors. Overwhelmingly, however, slaves would kinetically restore their beings as slaves in the same fashion as their counterparts would enact their positions as white oppressors. The former would perpetually choose to be bond in a field of possibilities that consisted variously of maligned corpse, perilously unsuccessful renegade, and accessory to familiacide and ambicide (as slaves' actions endangered also the lives of their beloved).

If we establish meaningful points of convergence between Gordon, West, and Sartre, then it is clear that choice of being is, inevitably, a function of the predicament into which one is "thrown" (adopting Heidegger's lexicon). In other words, one's fundamental choice is forged not so much as the solipsistic byproduct of consciousness, but rather at the intersubjective nexus of consciousness and circumstance. This summation does not account for the ways in which choice importunes one to be in the quotidian—that register of life that exists apart from the dramatic rupture, in which the other possibilities in the field conspicuously assert their presence or, in rare cases, their plausibility. Sartre calculated that this stratum of existence involved, for the Parisian citizens, "living," which exists somewhere between half-hatred and amicability, and teleological projection toward a state of freedom and the position of "wanted" men and women.

Many have brilliantly analyzed the discursive practices of Africana peoples as fertile sites of inquiry into this "living."[16] In his analysis of postcolonial Cameroonian society, Achille Mbembe is particularly eloquent on this point, especially the ways in which discursivity (as a window into living) occurs in the intersubjective nexus of consciousness and a founding societal logic (1992). Mbembe hails this founding logic *commandement*, a French term that denotes colonial authority, particularly its instantiation as institutional and semiotic structures of hegemony, and public symbols of grandeur to which all are expected to offer due obeisance. For Mbembe, what lends the postcolony its particular character is the cohabitation of dominant and dominated within the system of *commandement*. Inside this system, the black African does not simply choose the being of dominated, but very often chooses to be, what Mbembe calls, "homo ludens," or "the one who plays." For homo ludens, verbal parody of *commandement*—with its inclination to excessive displays of power—constitutes a type of provincial colloquy. What must be noted, however, is that, despite his or her parodic aptitude, homo ludens never subverts the dominant societal logic, or achieves social ascendancy. In fact, homo ludens' very choice of being could not ever manifest itself without the governing logic of *commandement*. The vernacular register of homo ludens, replete with obscenity and grotesquery, is a mirror image of the grand excesses of colonial powers (e.g., elaborate inaugural ceremonies, public displays of violence and terror, broad-scale pillages, and elaborate protocols of showing deference). Mbembe sums up this total situation as the "banality of power in the postcolony."

Certainly "banality" appropriately names the general existential situation of Africana peoples historically (I am excluding the martyr and the consummate revolutionary here). For in uttering that term, one simultaneously communicates the various degrees of density of a hierarchical symbolic order, and the exhaustion that an Africana subject experiences from recuperating (never undoing) that order regimentally.

Conclusions

The insights of Africana existentialists offer much to extend Sartre's existential psychoanalysis, particularly for understanding the predicament of Africana peoples historically. The colonial and post-colonial encounters between whiteness and blackness allow us to understand the ways in which fundamental projects are formed intersubjectively and dialectically, rather than hermetically. Furthermore, the intercourse of these disparate positions teaches us that a subject always chooses provisionally, as s/he is never exempt from the kinetic and mutually negating/constituting conditions of bad and good faith. For Africana peoples, a hierarchical symbolic order and its co-constitutive corporeal, psychoanalytic and social realities construct an intersubjective field of possible beings, from which the subject may choose. In the antebellum period, Africana peoples generally (dare I say) chose to be slaves rather than risk the torture and death of themselves and their loved ones. In the present day, the possibilities for Africana being have been enumerated (although some have remained constant: the danger of being conscripted for slave labor, threats of race-related violence and death, negative evaluations of self, and inferior social positionality among others), yet all exist within an enduring symbolic order and under the pall of what Gordon calls "oppression."

The question arises then: Why is it even necessary to understand one's positionality as a choice or a fundamental project, when it is clear that circumstance is the force that compels a particular project into existence, circumscribes it and dictates, in many respects, how it will be "lived"? After all, many have argued quite convincingly that the racist political order has proven its intransigence.

What a focus on the fundamental project allows us to see are people who, in choosing to live, are condemned to always commit the act of choosing how they will live, regardless of the nature of the situation in which they are embedded. We are presented with subjects who are perpetually awake, aware, sentient, and enterprising. So, even if there are those living in a state of postmodern ennui, they are damned to experience it, not as an absence of interest, but rather as a sensation of perpetually jettisoning intrigue. It is this stratum of living, which I have named tropological density, that I find of particular interest for subaltern subjects. In essence, this living, or the tropologically dense field into which the subject emerges, is not truly distinguishable from whom these subjects are becoming. Stated another way, living and becoming represent differing emphases upon a single ontological genesis; living emphasizes the actual occurrence of that genesis, while becoming emphasizes the outcomes, which occur iteratively.

At this terminal juncture, it now becomes clear that ontogenesis at the level of the individual is analogous to, and a part of, the dialectical ontogenesis of history itself. This statement would seem to maintain its integrity whether applied to Africana life-worlds or others. If what I have said up to this point has any merit at all, then an existential psychoanalytic project that functions at the level of the individual should offer profound insight into the sociocultural predicament into which individuals arrive, and analyses of the sociocultural ought to illuminate the ways in which individuals live and become, as asymptotically impossible as the completion of either of these objectives must eternally remain.

EXISTENTIAL PSYCHOANALYTIC ANTHROPOLOGY: FUNDAMENTAL PROJECTION AND THE MECHANISMS OF CONSCIOUSNESS

As I stated in the beginning, this has been an elaborate exercise in way clearing. I first made an argument for a serious consideration of consciousness, both as object and subject of scientific inquiry. I then made a case for a distinctly anthropological theory of consciousness that could have broad trans-disciplinary currency. I then proceeded to enumerating the features of such a theory, explicating the mechanisms of consciousness, concentrating on the operational values of cognition and affect. Next, I demonstrated how a consideration of Sartre and the Africana existentialists could contribute to our understanding of these mechanisms of cognition and affect. All that remains now are some concluding remarks about how to achieve a rapprochement between the hermetic and intersubjective varieties of existential psychoanalysis, and anthropology of cognition and affect. Stated differently, I would like to consider the reciprocal influence of fundamental projection and the mechanisms of consciousness.

The first matter at hand is the reciprocal constitution of fundamental projection and symbolization, the foundational mechanism of cognition. If we choose who we become among culturally defined possibles, and if this procedure occurs intersubjectively, does this projection inform the manner in which cognition makes use of symbols? I would contend that the very onto-logical structure of that fundamental choice is symbolic—it consists of par-ticular accretions of meaning and systems of accretion. The fact that this choice is inaccessible is consonant with the fact that the symbolic configura-tions operate on the pre-objective plane (Sartre's critique of Freudian meta-theory prohibits me from referring to this pre-objectivity as unconscious). That this choice is compelling is consistent with the fact that symbolic con-figurations reverberate throughout psychic, affective, and physiological reg-isters, effecting actual subjective and intersubjective transformations. From Sartre and the Africana existentialists, we glean that circumstance, which includes the intersubjective play of projects, places constraints upon how a single project can and will be instituted.[17] This idea echoes what anthropolo-gists have always known about the defining influence of culture. Sartre's observations about the French Occupation and the Africana existentialists' regarding trans-Atlantic colonization of Africana subjects are particularly telling, however. Both suggest that alterations in fundamental choices are most definitive when there are architectonic shifts in life-worlds and cosmol-ogies. One recalls here Durkheim's and Turner's observations about the transformative nature of ritual, the hallmark of which is its excess, oddity, and, in some cases, perdurance—the outcome of which is a seismic, irrevo-cable shift in the psyches of those involved (Olaveson 2001). Thus, what the existentialists knew about defining historical moments, Turner and Durkheim observed about ritual. In sum, I would contend that fundamental projection is the Ur mechanism by which meanings accrete into symbols, symbols organize themselves into pre-objective and objective systems, and these congeries of meanings become personally and culturally resonant.

Resonance not only occurs at the level of symbolicity, but of emotion also. The resonance of symbols mirrors the epiphenomenality of affect. I would go so far as to argue that affect itself is one mode of the symbolic reverberations that individuals experience. Thus, affective reverberations are the direct result of the fundamental choice of being, which itself, epiphenom-enally and iteratively, compels distinct modes of cognition and affect. That emotion is a manner of sociocultural comportment is consistent with funda-mental projection's dual nature as intuitively felt, yet inaccessible. For, com-porting oneself to a situation, as Sartre and many anthropologists of con-sciousness would agree, tends to occur at the limen of pre-objectivity and objectivity, in a condition of processual and phenomenological immediacy. In short, fundamental projection is the epicentric mechanism that drives the epiphenomenality and comportmentality of affect.

Continuing in the present spirit of synthesis, I would like to offer a concluding note about the composite value of experience itself. While I am invested wholeheartedly in the phenomenological project, I am inclined to agree with Desjarlais that terms such as "experience" and "phenomenological reality" tend to obscure what really occurs at the interface of cognition, affect, sensation, culture, and society. If we are to have a rigorous anthropological science of consciousness, then we must continue to disaggregate and operationalize composite values, search for mechanisms, and continue to allow both of these processes to continue their ongoing dialogue with the *interpreted* facts of the ethnographic record. It is only by adhering to these methodological cautions that anthropological theories of consciousness can gain trans-disciplinary currency.

NOTES

1. Refer to *Logical Investigations* (1970) for a fuller understanding of Husserl's phenomenological method.

2. See the opening chapter of *Being and Nothingness* (1993).

3. This particular article provides a useful corrective to misinterpretations of Husserl's method.

4. In "Anthropology and the Savage Slot: The Poetics and Politics of Otherness" (1991), Trouillot offers a stunning account of the cultural, discursive, and historical mechanisms that instituted this particular "disciplining" of anthropology.

5. It must also be noted that this "insistence" has always been attended by the problematizing of cultural boundaries and the very concept of "culture" itself.

6. I use the term "laboratory" very loosely. Along with other anthropologists, I recognize the inadequacies of a purely experimental model for evaluating social phenomena.

7. For Tylor and the other evolutionists, this error was inevitable in societies that had not yet emerged from what were called the "savage" or "barbaric" stages.

8. One is reminded here of the totemic variety of Durkheim's "collective representations"—which emerge as overdetermined symbols of the social group itself that subsequently impress themselves powerfully upon the minds and hearts of all members within that social group (*The Elementary Forms of Religious Life*).

9. In "Embodiment as a Paradigm for Anthropology" (1990), Csordas performs a similar procedure by arguing for the irreducibility of a phenomenological experience/culture dyad.

10. By "arbitrary," I mean an act of privileged authority, not its colloquial gloss, "random." For Geertz would insist that the content of this act of arbitration is culturally informed.

11. I do not here mean to suggest that these patterns are always regular and congruous. Refer to Sally Falk Moore's *Symbol and Politics in Communal Ideology* (1976) for a discussion of the priority of indeterminacy in cultural arrangements.

12. This particular observation is relatively commonsensical in anthropological discourse, as, in cultures worldwide, that which defies categories tends to be regarded as a monstrosity, scapegoat, pariah, or witch. The uncanny and the monstrous are analogous to those entities that emerge within what Victor Turner calls the "liminal" stages of social processes, the anti-structure. See Turner's *The Ritual Process: Structure and Anti-Structure* (1969).

13. It must be noted here that Mimica, like Jackson (2012), appears to use the term "phenomenological" as synonymous with emic categories of cognition and affect. It is debatable

whether such a slippage is warranted, given that phenomenology itself has a philosophical history distinct from that of the cultures being studied.

14. This is an insight borrowed from Nussbaum (2001).

15. Gordon uses this term to refer to all peoples of African descent, regardless of national background. Thus, the designation includes African-descended people in Europe, the United States, Latin America and any other location containing African-descended people. This point is particularly important, given that the position of African-descended peoples in the symbolic order is globally resonant.

16. See Henry L. Gates, *Signifying Monkey: A Theory of Afro-American Literary Criticism* (New York: Oxford University Press, 1988), and Nathaniel Mackey, *Discrepant Engagement: Dissonance, Cross-Culturality, and Experimental Writing* (New York: Cambridge University Press, 1993).

17. This idea is consistent with C. Jason Throop's discussion of one of the existential structures that mediate experience and extra-mental reality, obduracy, which refers to the "quality of reality to resist the will and intentionality of the psyche" (Throop and Laughlin 2009).

Chapter Two

From *Plessy* to NCLB

The "Peculiar" Practice of Segregation in American Public Education

The passage of the No Child Left Behind Act (NCLB) at the dawn of the twenty-first century is intimately connected to the long and contentious history of black-white race relations in the United States. Since the founding of America, African Americans have engaged in an epic struggle to claim a sense of humanity in the face of institutions that had legal sanction to negate it. Defining blacks as three-fifths of a human being provided a legal justification for the "peculiar institution" of slavery and a long history of physical, psychological, emotional, and hermeneutic violence against them. With the legal abolition of slavery in 1865, black Americans seemed poised to finally lay claim to all the rights and advantages of "full" human beings. This prospect appeared to be even more feasible with the ratification of the Fourteenth Amendment, which forbade states from denying its citizens equal protection under the law. However, in the landmark court case *Plessy v. Ferguson* (1896), the Supreme Court ruled that the separation of the races did not necessarily imply the inferiority of blacks to whites (163 U.S. 537). By instituting the legally sanctioned separation of the races, the Supreme Court reinstalled the common structure of racial subordination and discrimination that had been undone (at least judicially) just thirty-two years earlier.

"Separate but equal," while an optimistic theory, was simply an untenable social and political solution. The sphere of education reflects this reality most profoundly. By mid-century, around 40 percent of all American students attended segregated schools. Black schools were significantly poorer than those of their white counterparts, and the former's buildings frequently appraised at values appreciably lower than those of white school buildings. In

Clarendon County, South Carolina, for example, the per-pupil expenditures in the years 1949 to 1950 averaged $179 for white students, yet only $43 for black students. This situation was mirrored in teacher salaries. Teachers in all black schools were paid approximately one-third less than those in white schools (Friedman 2008).

The Supreme Court decision of 1954 to render segregated schools unconstitutional marked a turning point in public education and race relations at large. *Brown v. Board of Education of Topeka Kansas* was a watershed moment not only because it cast a decisive blow to American segregation, but also because it extended federal power to education, which had traditionally been the domain of states and localities (347 U.S. 483). The outlawing of segregation in the schools was not enough to permanently undo practices that had been entrenched in American society for hundreds of years, however. Nevertheless, these landmark court decisions, along with other legal efforts, did advance the goal of full social integration. A reverberation of the *Brown* decision, the Civil Rights Act of 1964 banned the administration of federal aid to schools that practiced racial segregation (42 U.S.C. 1971). Other court cases such as *Green v. County School Board of New Kent County* (391 U.S. 430), which stipulated that desegregation must occur immediately, hastened the purported equalizing of educational opportunities for black students. As a result of *Brown* and subsequent legal interventions, numerous school districts across the country were placed under mandatory segregation plans. The era of widespread school desegregation had been set into motion.

While desegregation plans established the groundwork for improving educational prospects for the country's disadvantaged students, the Elementary and Secondary Education Act, which President Lyndon B. Johnson signed into existence in 1965, was intended to provide a fiscal budget for these reforms. The centerpiece of this legislation was "Title I," which apportioned $1.06 billion in "financial assistance . . . to expand and improve . . . educational programs by various means . . . which contribute particularly to meeting the special educational needs of educationally deprived children" (Spring 1976). With school desegregation well under way and the federal government pouring money into the education of its black citizenry, black students were destined to achieve educational parity with white students. Yet this parity has not occurred. Why?

The short answer is that the federal government has not maintained its allegiance to the goal of educational parity. Between the mid-1970s and 1990, no significant Supreme Court rulings were made with regard to school integration. This period of relative latency, therefore, allowed for the beginning of another trend. School districts were beginning to deem desegregation plans passé, and started getting legal justification to abort them. As a result of their active petitioning, school boards in Oklahoma (498 U.S. 237) and Missouri (515 U.S. 70, 1995) in 1991 and 1992, respectively, were released from court order to continue their previously instituted desegregation plans. These court cases served as legal precedents, accelerating exemption from desegregation plans in school districts across the country (Tushnet 1996). According to many researchers, the result of this counter trend is that many schools and districts across the nation have become effectively resegregated (Eaton and Orfield 1996; Boger 2002; Frankenberg, Lee, and Orfield 2003; Lutz 2005). This same body of research also presents compelling evidence of the correlation between the current trend toward resegregation and the failed educational outcomes of blacks and other minority students.

The No Child Left Behind Act of 2001 built upon Title I of the Elementary and Secondary Education Act (ESEA) of 1965 to expand the latter's accountability and assessment requirements (Eisner et al. 2007). Every child was to make "adequate yearly progress" (AYP) in math and English Language Arts. The ultimate goal was that 100 percent of the nation's children would achieve proficiency in these areas by 2014 (U.S. Department of Education, Office of Planning, Evaluation and Policy Development, Policy and Program Studies Service 2009). This particular mandate was purported to narrow the achievement gap between the nation's disadvantaged and privileged—a gap that happens to be the result of several decades of discriminatory practices. However, modest gains in the area of test performance in no way fulfill the root intention of NCLB and its legislative antecedents: to provide equal educational opportunities for all students (Johnson 2005).

While students in wealthier school districts and those attending private schools (it must be noted that the latter group is predominantly white) enjoy high-caliber teachers and well-rounded curriculums, students in Title I schools—those schools with a majority of students who are minority, learning disabled or immigrant—languish under the strict demands of accountability regimens. The cycle goes as follows. In order for the school to stay open and receive federal funding, its students must achieve AYP (which is primarily determined through state-administered standardized tests). To ensure that students achieve high marks on the tests, the school-day curriculum is inundated with excessive periods of math and English Language Arts, to the marginalization and/or total exclusion of other subject matter. The result is that many teachers become uninspired to teach, students become resistant to learning, and the students' educational experiences become severely limited (Poetter 2004, 2006; Bird 2006). This cycle has adverse consequences not only for a student's educational prospects, but also for his/her total being. Students are deprived of the critical connections between experiencing and learning (Howard 2006) and fail to receive the tools to achieve an overall sense of personal fulfillment and well-being (Parmigian 2006).

The obvious paradox here is that the very children whom the No Child Left Behind Act purportedly helps are the ones whom the legislation most adversely affects. Coupled with the, by now, national orthodoxy of anti-desegregation efforts (as desegregation plans have now been coded as instances of reverse racism) (Lindseth 2002), NCLB has not only accelerated the effective resegregation of the public school system, but it has also ensured that America's disadvantaged children remain educationally deprived. Ostensibly a legal code that provides a vision of optimism for our nation's youth—all children achieving proficiency in math and literacy by 2014—proves, in reality, to be little more than an apocalyptic reinstatement of *Plessy*.

Yet, one wonders how NCLB assumed its particular form. What made high-stakes testing, rigid systems of accountability, and punitive regulation of school's progress the norm? How did these particular matters come to be emphasized over and beyond the virtues of "good teaching," "nurturing the whole child," producing well-rounded citizens of a thriving democracy? One answer lies in the role that America's public education system has played in domestic and international political games.

PUBLIC EDUCATION AND AMERICAN ELECTORAL POLITICS FROM 1965-2001

In *No Child Left Behind and the Transformation of Federal Education Policy, 1965-2005*, Patrick McGuinn advances the argument that the eventual emergence of NCLB was the result of America's presidential electoral politics. He grounds his argument in the premise that, in a society such as the United States, which undergoes frequently occurring elections, electoral candidates are inevitably compelled to address shifts in national public policy demands.

Prior to the 1950s, the topic of education was not considered a national issue in the United States. In fact, "education" is never mentioned in the U.S. Constitution. Unlike with other polities around the world, education has been traditionally the domain of state and local governments, with little federal intervention. This scenario saw a seismic shift mid-century, due to issues in the domestic and international spheres, however.

As mentioned earlier, the *Brown* ruling, which was instrumental in ending legal segregation in schools, brought the topic of education to the forefront of the national political agenda. Coupled with the subsequent passage of the Civil Rights Act of 1965, *Brown* also became instrumental in prompting hyper-awareness of civil rights more generally (Guthrie 1983). Fueling the public consciousness around these issues was a proliferation of research concerning social inequalities.

Added to domestic concerns over educational equality and social parity was a serious consideration of how the United States was faring with other nations around the world, particularly the Soviet Union. Cold War politics fueled inevitable tensions and competition between the U.S. and U.S.S.R., a situation which was played out in the realm of education. The 1950s launch of the world's first orbiting satellite, Sputnik, left the United States with the impression that it was falling behind technologically and militaristically. As a result, America became particularly anxious about the state of its educational system. For lags in technology were assumed to be the direct result of a comparatively inferior educational structure.

Sputnik and *Brown v. Board of Education* made education one of the top public policy concerns of the 1950s and 1960s. President Lyndon B. Johnson, vice presidential successor to John F. Kennedy, capitalized on the new environment of social awareness and international competition by advancing a platform that sought to eliminate poverty and its root causes. Johnson waged an internecine "war on poverty" and thrust civil rights to the forefront of the domestic agenda. Johnson maintained that "very often, a lack of jobs and money is not the cause of poverty, but the symptom. The cause may lie deeper—in our failure to give our fellow citizens a fair chance to develop their own capacities in a lack of education and training" (Jeffrey 1978). The natural progression of Johnson's agenda, therefore, was to introduce an education plan that would offer American citizens a "fifth freedom": "freedom from ignorance" (Howe 1990). In 1965, Johnson was able to push for the Elementary and Secondary Education Act, which would offer federal aid to school districts that were actively pursuing desegregation plans. As has already been stated, Title I of the act was explicitly aimed at enhancing the educational prospects of the nation's most disadvantaged children. Title I raised per-pupil expenditures as a way of making a direct investment in the education of individuals in the under-class.

According to McGuinn, this was the first moment in history in which the federal government had such an intimate involvement with the national education system. Yet, the remnants of a laissez faire approach to American education continued to persist. While more federal dollars were being poured into school districts, and particularly into the education of poor African Americans, state and local school districts had jurisdiction over how these monetary infusions were distributed. With increased financing did not come a commensurate increase in standards and expectations for how the money would be spent.

This lack of accountability eventually became a downfall. In the 1970s and 1980s, concerns mounted that, despite federal intervention, America's public education system was shown to be deteriorating. In 1983, the release of the national report *A Nation at Risk* exacerbated the growing discontent with the declining educational system. Based on comparative international data, this report argued convincingly that America was falling behind other nations, particularly the U.S.S.R., in educational achievement. The report conveyed the message that, in order for our nation's youth to improve their educational standing, and hence the degraded state of the country, greater systems of educational accountability were necessary (National Commission on Excellence in Education 1983). In the era after ESEA, therefore, the voting public came to see the federal government—particularly what came to be seen as its irresponsible spending practice with regard to education—as the culprit in a failing educational system.

In the 1980 and 1984 presidential elections, President Ronald Reagan was able to use public disapproval of the federal government's role in education to his advantage. He insisted that because the federal government's involvement with public institutions of learning since the 1960s had proven ineffective, it was time for deregulation of public education and social welfare systems more generally. This rhetoric, in many ways, guaranteed two successful presidential elections. During Reagan's administration federal funding for public education decreased sharply, and the National Department of Education—which Reagan was seeking to completely dismantle—was significantly downsized (Clark and Verstegan 1988).

Yet many did not favor Reagan's platform. Publicizing the epic failures of American education, Reagan did not succeed in convincing citizens that federal intervention was the enemy. His rhetoric backfired. People became convinced that federal spending was necessary, yet needed to be accompanied by appropriate national leadership. Although he was unsuccessful in his attempts to demonize federal educational spending and the national Department of Education, Reagan did manage to undermine the position that mere access to education (the result of federal spending) would ensure increased achievement. More and more American citizens became convinced that in addition to access, students needed more rigorous academic standards. By the end of the 1980s, therefore, it was clear that if the federal government were to intervene into the affairs of school districts, it would have to do so in a way that was more directed and specific.

If Reagan, through a negative feedback loop, inadvertently persuaded Americans that federal spending on education was indispensable, the subsequent presidency of George H. W. Bush, through similar inadvertence, fixed this position more firmly in the minds of the American public. Like Reagan, Bush advocated rollbacks in federal education spending. And, as with Reagan, Bush encountered much more opposition to his policies than he did support.

By the end of Bush's presidency, American citizens more than ever were convinced that what public education needed were more rigor, leadership and specificity in educational spending. Bill Clinton's advocacy of these protocols contributed greatly to his victories in the 1992 and 1996 presidential elections. By the end of his two terms in office, Clinton had managed to garner massive appropriations for education from a majority Republican Congress (which had historically opposed federal spending in education) and had stewarded the most dramatic increase in K–12 spending that the country had seen since the 1960s (National Center for Education Statistics, 2002).

By 2000, therefore, the groundwork had been thoroughly prepared for a political platform that not only advocated considerable federal spending on education, but also federal oversight of how this fiscal investment would be directed. In fact, education became one of the most prominent issues in the 2000 elections. It has even been argued that the undue attention that George W. Bush devoted to matters of education accounts for his initial victory (Winston 2003). By the time Bush junior had taken office, momentum had gathered behind the issue of restructuring federal educational policy. The new reform was to include the many lessons that had been learned since the 1960s. The federal government would make sizable fiscal investments in the nation's underachieving students, while ensuring that these dollars were distributed with rigorous assessment standards (Nather 2001). The result was the signing of NCLB into law in 2001.

Yet between the federal distribution of funds to public school districts to enforce accountability standards, and how school districts redistribute funds and enforce these standards, there is a conspicuous absence of accountability. For instance, one of the most significant indices of per student expenditure is teacher salary. Experienced, veteran teachers invariably earn much more than teachers who are newer to the profession. These veterans tend to be lured away to higher achieving, higher paying schools, leaving Title I schools with a preponderance of novice teachers. This situation only serves to exacerbate the proverbial "achievement gap." Because school districts are only required to report averages in spending per pupil (a significant part of which is teacher salaries) to justify receipt of federal dollars, underachieving students in Title I schools continue to receive considerably less than their wealthier counterparts (Spatig-Amerikaner 2012). In short, there is no system in place to ensure that Title I students actually receive the resources they require to meet their educational needs.

Additionally, there is overwhelming evidence that NCLB's ironic lack of accountability has encouraged schools to practice educational "triage," or the process by which teachers offer more attention to those students who directly affect accountability ratings (Booher-Jennings 2006; Springer 2005). According to Booher-Jennings's study of Title I schools in Texas, teachers not only concentrated their efforts on students who had a chance of passing the state examinations, but would refer the other children to special education classes. In one notable study of Chicago public schools, principals themselves were encouraging teachers to nurture the academic growth of students who were close to passing or had a considerable chance of passing state examinations (Youdell and Gillborn 2000; Youdell 2004).

In short, what is justified as a solution to the United States' educational and social problems is, in reality, those problems' precipitate. Moreover, what masquerades as educational accountability standards is little more than an increase in the mere *rhetoric* of accountability.

CONCLUSIONS

From the foregoing discussion, it is clear that the current state of education is, to a partial degree, the result of political self-interest and maneuvering. High-stakes testing, the mandate of "adequate yearly progress" in the areas of math and literacy, and the targeting of Title I schools for federal funding have merited two sets of winners, with one conspicuous loser: political candidates have taken offices, the economies of school districts have received generous subsidies, yet high-need student populations have sunken into deeper levels of disadvantage and been deprived of a quality education.

In many ways, the current state of urban education is the symptom of a question that has persisted since the cessation of the Civil War: What is the country to do with millions of manumitted slaves? The Freedman's Bureau was little more than an ambitious failure, as it was simply not feasible that a country would deprive an entire group of civil and human rights, capital and human dignity and expect that an ill-conceived, haphazard plan would rectify the situation. *Plessy* was destined to be a failure in this same regard. *Brown*, which laid the groundwork for social parity, and ESEA and President Johnson's overall vision for reducing educational and civil disparities were leading the country in the right direction. In the present era of NCLB, the hereditary and political descendants of those manumitted millions are still languishing under policies that blatantly undermine the spirit of their own articulation. As a result, minority students continue to dwell within an existential predicament of oppression, expendability, and confiscated humanity.

Chapter Three

Four-Dimensionality and the Ironic

In New York City, the physical architecture of a school is barely distinguishable from that of any other building. The school building is connected, indissociably, to all the other edifices on a city block: apartment complexes, bodegas, business offices, restaurants, and the like. You know that you have arrived at a school building by one of a few different physical indicators. You may stumble upon a playground that is completely embroidered with a tall metal fence, for instance. The equipment will almost always communicate the grand abstraction "color"—lots of color. Each color will achieve its cathexis with a particular object and stand in blaring contrast to the other color-enveloped objects in the quad—a profusion of reds, greens, yellows, and blues. One would never encounter the mere insinuation of color—pastels, beiges, sky blues—the absence of color—white—and certainly, one would never see color in its most grotesque, saturated form: black. One would only see something reminiscent of what we assume to be the Technicolor universe of a child's imagination. Yet you would only see this universe if you happened to peer through the near opacity of the fence that occupies only about twenty seconds of a typical city block. Otherwise, you would never know that a playground or a school were present.

You might also know that you have encountered a school if you pay attention to the subtleties of architecture. Above the door of almost every school building in New York there is an almost imperceptible concrete design. Lodged in the midst of this design you will see a couple of letters followed by one to three numbers: for example, PS 12 or MS 141, which stand for, respectively, "Public School 12" or "Middle School 141." If you happen to notice the design or the inscriptions, then you know for certain that you have arrived at a public school building.

Upon entering The Academy, I was greeted by three entities. The first two were darkness and its corollary, narrowness. There was what seemed like one source of electric light hovering only dimly above the small enclosure that served as an entryway into the rest of the building. It was not designed for human habitation, necessarily. The space was too tight and lightless to accommodate social gatherings. And, because it had no décor or other objects to enchant a conscious being, the space provided no topics for conversation. The abundant absences of the space were essentially hostile to any possibility of social existence.

The third entity I encountered was a security officer, a woman of rather friendly and accommodating demeanor. The first three days of my visit she asked me to procure my driver's license and amicably directed me to The Academy. Each day I signed in and proceeded to my destination. After the third day of my visit, she only asked me to sign the security registry and told me to enjoy my day. The journey to my ultimate destination was as forbidding as my entry to the building. I had to endure four flights of stairs to reach the top floor. Along the way, I passed an elementary school and a middle school, each assigned to its own floor.

When I reached the top of the stairs, again, I found myself in a dark, narrow void. One would not even know that he or she had entered the space of a school if it were not for the stream of children that would be passing through at about 8 a.m. There were no signs acknowledging one's arrival to The Academy, such as there was for Randolph, which was only two floors below. At Randolph, there was a large, gleaming, prodigious sign that read "Randolph School," which included a byline that attested to the excellence of the institution. At The Academy, what one met upon arriving was the fully abundant absence of grandeur. The vacuity was made even more plentiful by the proximity of its opposite. The doors to Randolph were equally as prodigious as the sign adorning them. Large double doors granted one entry into a glimmering, expansive hallway, the floors of which looked as if they had been buffed for hours.

Beyond the narrow entryway of The Academy, by contrast, was a gymnasium, which had an area that was but a small fraction of that of a gym in a more reputable school. The Academy's gymnasium had a luster commensurate with its compromised size. The floors were exceptionally dull and brown. The bleachers were brown. The basketball goals had white and black backboards with rusted orange hoops. The space was a grand transgression of all the rules applicable to an outdoor playground. Present were the negations of color, adornment, and imagination. From the upstairs entryway to the gym, no signs of vibrancy, hospitableness, or prodigiousness were inscribed into the floors or the walls or the ceilings. Both spaces were sparsely illuminated with weak electric lights. Neither were there any windows to admit light from outside. To get to the school proper, one had to go through the gymnasium (a ritual highly unconventional even for a Title I school).

As soon as you opened the doors to leave the gymnasium, you knew that you were in the main part of the school. Stretching your arms wide like an eagle, you were able to touch both walls of the inordinately narrow main hallway. The first room on the left was the administrative office. Also along that hallway were Mr. Wheeler's science classroom and Mrs. Beal's English classroom. The end of the rather short hallway abruptly split in two directions. Taking either route would send one on a somewhat frightening journey to what seemed like some forbidden destination. Each route was a passageway even narrower than the one previously mentioned. It winded several times, around sharp, unpredictable corners, until finally it terminated in another classroom or an exit. A bathroom might be positioned, inconsequentially, along the maze-route. There were no windows along the narrow corridors. The standard electric light fixtures on the ceilings emitted only a sinister, mocking luminosity, ultimately daunted by the darkening effects of opposing walls that hastened toward a common center.

Educational studies confirm what our common sense might recommend about the effects of such desolation upon the moods and overall performance of its daily inhabitants. Pamela Woolner offers compelling evidence that well-lit school environments improve both the mood and productivity of the students (Woolner et al. 2007). By contrast, those settings that are more darkly lit tend to have the obverse effect (Knez 1995; Jago and Tanner 1999). One body of scholarship proposes that an abundance of natural "daylight" improves academic performance (Heschong Mahone Group 2003; Earthman 2004). Other findings even suggest that there is a direct causal link between inadequate and flickering lights and such physiological issues such as headaches, eyestrain, and fatigue (Karpen 1993; Barnitt 2003).

"Build quality" of the school also significantly affects both students' and teachers' perceptions of the space (Tanner, 2000). Higher ceilings, for instance, give teachers and students the feeling that a classroom is less crowded, with the height of the ceiling correlating significantly with teachers' overall sense of satisfaction with classrooms (Ahrentzen and Evans 1984).

The overall aesthetic landscape of the built environment is also not to be discounted as powerfully evocative of particular moods. Maxwell's study uncovers that students formulate definite opinions about whether they feel welcomed or repelled by the colors around them (2000). Burke and Grosvenor indicate that children tend to prefer color, as opposed to its absence (2003). Hallam suggests that a school environment that is perceived to be generally unattractive begins a chain reaction beginning with "affect": students experience a decline in their moods; they are discouraged from entering the space at all; attendance rates drop; and truancy rates soar (1996). Maslow and Mintz (1956) found that indecorous spaces tend to evoke more negative judgments than "beautiful spaces." Finally, Sommer and Olsen (1980) and Berry (2002) found that new buildings and the renovation of old ones significantly improve students' motivation and engagement.

As could be predicted, the foregoing studies are commensurate with the testimonies of the students and faculty in The Academy. A conversation with one of the attending students, an African American girl named Jessica, may serve to extend our comprehension of the intricate ways that physical space articulates with students' phenomenological encounters with their school.

Me: "How do you like your school?"

Jessica: "This school needs work!"

Me: "What kind of work?"

Jessica: "It needs paint on the walls. Put the names of the students who go here and who have been here!"

Me: "Why should the school do this?"

Jessica: "I don't know. Just to have art on the walls."

When asked her opinion of her school, Jessica immediately referenced its physicality. Yet, for her the physicality of the school was innately layered with other meanings and suggestions. Jessica had already been inducted into a symbolic system in which fresh paint, artwork, and the inscription of students' names were cemented to the semantic unit, "desired appearance."[1] It is this fundamental accretion of meanings that "resonates"[2] in particular ways, and makes other phenomenological configurations inevitable for Jessica: the judgment that the present space was undesirable, and a viscerally affective sense of aversion. And yet, the architecture of this symbolic system and Jessica's aversion to it are a bit more complex. "Work," for Jessica, suggested a deliberate effort to maintain and construct the environment in ways that would be satisfying to its inhabitants. Painted walls and artwork both spoke to conventions that one would normally find in New York's more well-kept schools. Because Jessica was generally aware of these conventions, the physical appearance of the walls was not simply a customary feature of the culture that she knew well and within which she was routinely immersed. The walls were not silent or unadorned, if we subscribe to sensory conceits. The walls were rife with holographic designs. The paint was on the walls, but in holographic form. The artwork, too, was hung along the perimeter of the walls, yet in diaphanous assertions of its absence. Everywhere Jessica looked, she was ridiculed, assaulted by these subliminal frames of non-being.

And what of the names of the students? Jessica emphasized the present perfect marker "have" as she expressed her desire to see names of students on the walls. The present perfect marker, indicative of a past that is inextricably linked to and has consequences for the present moment, connected Jessica to her scholastic ancestors. The "have" sutured her to a present that was the cumulative product of several historical progressions, consisting of people and circumstances. But alas, if the "have" be a nexus between the past and the present, only the latter half of the totality possessed a being. Yet, nestled within the present were the fecund seeds of its own undoing. For that present was not grafted into the architecture of the school. The names of the students "who go here" were holographically inscribed along the walls, and so were the artistic products of human presence. Everywhere Jessica looked she was presented with the pall of ahistoricity and the prophecy of a vanished present. Jessica knew that she and the other students who were occupying the school would not be memorialized along its walls. The present moment and her own existence were both a part of the same holograph—present in its inveterate procedures of departing.

Jessica's visceral need to see these walls covered over with names, paint, and artwork escaped her ability to explain "why" the school should have made these types of investments. If we admit that our ability to explicate and critically evaluate mitigate the potency of unpropitious circumstances, I wonder about the extent of Jessica's aversion to her surroundings. How often did she experience displeasure as a result of merely attending school? What were the particular regions of the physical space that accosted her? How did her displeasure affect other regions of experience? To what extent was her daily encounter with The Academy both pre-objective and objective?

To say that Jessica was experiencing displeasure because her environment lacked the virtue of pulchritude would be a gross simplification. For the built space itself, an agentive subject in its own right, was engaged with Jessica in a recurring, kinetic exchange. The walls calculated her value and articulated this quantity to her. In other words, if we recall insights from chapter 1, Yancy, Manganyi, and Mbembe offer us an alternative way with which to read Jessica's predicament: she and the physical space of the school began to achieve their respective beings intersubjectively. Those spectral projections whispered to her that neither she nor her schoolmates were worthy of recognition or of the luxuries afforded to Randolph. They were all regarded as disposable features of their institution, and, by prophetic extension, the institutions they would one day encounter in the larger society.

And these walls spoke with such conviction—the certitude of an interlocutor endorsed by the right of a fiduciary system of metrics. Indeed, Jessica had been deemed unworthy of the investment. For she attended what is known as an "under-resourced school," a descriptor that is typically taken to be synonymous with the term "Title I School." As Frank Adamson and Linda

Darling-Hammond suggest, resources play an integral role in a school's ability to enhance the academic prospects of its students (2011). Under Title I of the Elementary and Secondary Education Act, school districts are required to provide funding equitably between the schools in its district. Once these districts demonstrate funding comparability, they become eligible for federal supplemental funding. However, as indicated in chapter 2, funding inequities persist due to a loophole in this accountability measure. According to Ary Spatig-Amerikaner, school districts only have to report comparability averages (2012). Yet more experienced teachers are more likely to relocate to schools that have lower percentages of high-need children, and are able to command more substantial salaries. The end result is that schools with a higher percentage of "Title I students" also have a higher concentration of inexperienced teachers. Thus, resource disparities persist between Title I schools and their wealthier counterparts, unbeknownst to the federal government. Overall then, this loophole allows school districts to apportion less money to high-need schools, a situation which is not permitted under the current law (Spatig-Amerikaner 2012).

In this way, the law provides the very condition for its own transgression, both de facto and de jure. We are therefore prompted to think about the spectacularity of the juridical in the ways that Kamari Clarke has outlined (2011). In her ethnographic study of legal proceedings in Sierra Leone, Clarke understands the international tribunal as a stage on which the law is made into a spectacle, replete with affective resonance, to displace culpability. In her analysis, the African warlord is scapegoated as the perpetrator of heinous crimes against humanity. The testimonies of victims of war violence and those of child soldiers (who occupy an ambiguous position between victim and perpetrator) inspire righteous indignation within the local and international "audience" bearing witness to the events of the tribunal. The spectacle of law masks, however, the complicity of consumer lust for precious stones (e.g., diamonds) and the acquisitiveness of companies that cater to this economy of desire, and thereby ignore any imperative of humanitarian responsibility.

Within the context of education in the United States, the No Child Left Behind Act (NCLB) and the public rhetoric that surrounds it constitute a comparable juridical spectacle. Urban poor children, like victims of war crimes and child soldiers in Sierra Leone, become the objects of pity in the public discourse. Urban poverty, a crime-ridden environment, and a degraded system of cultural values, then, become the perpetrators of grave atrocities, ultimately, depriving children of adequate educational prospects. Within this economy of affect, in which responsibility assumes an inevitably bifurcated character, culpability is assigned unilaterally to the urban environment and children are the victims. This particular "narrative," in Clarke's lexicon, achieves legitimacy by what Bartolomé (1994) and Cross (2007) allude to as a process of assigning negative valuations as endemic to minority cultures. The authentic narrative concerning the root causes of educational underachievement becomes "encapsulated" (Clarke 2011) within a disingenuous narrative that is constructed dichotomously.[3] The result is an obfuscation of, what Cho and Lewis refer to as, "the real," which begs to be disclosed by some sort of "truth-event" (2005).

In the case of NCLB, the authentic "narrative," also "the real," is this: the educational disparity between ethnic minorities and their white counterparts is the result of a persistent racist symbolic order and racist institutional practices. It is no coincidence, for instance, that, in the present day, schools with predominantly black, Latina(o), and other ethnic minority attendants continue to be, since the era of legal segregation, underfunded, under-resourced, and academically challenged (refer to chapter 2). Or, stated another way, the relegation of minority students to inferior schools has been a compulsory practice since Jim Crow and is still occurring in the present day. Thus, Jessica and the other students who routinely confront the pallor of The Academy engage in an existential exchange with the adumbrations of a history that attempts to disavow its own historicity.

For the faculty members, the physical space of the school was also quite voluble. On a particular day of my attendance, I got a very rare opportunity to speak in-depth with Mrs. Black, an elderly white woman who was the appointed custodian of the student library. She offered much insight into the New York Public School System and how The Academy fits into that more encompassing structure: "At other schools, this [motioning to a disheveled classroom] would not happen. In private schools, there are squads in every class to keep order, to replace books on shelves, keep the room tidy." It is clear here that Mrs. Black was heir to the same symbolic agglomerations as Jessica; her phenomenological experience of the classroom was a flickering field of life-like illusions. For Mrs. Black, the same features that were in "other schools," which include "private schools," were also present at The Academy. The Academy had a "squad" of individuals who kept order in the classroom. When books were taken off or forcibly discharged from the shelves, the squad at The Academy would ensure that these items were replaced. Should the room fall into disarray, and tabletops become soiled with excess papers and broken utensils, the squad would discard these items. In fact, everywhere Mrs. Black looked in The Academy, order prevailed. All these elements were there, parading as spectral antipathies. As Mrs. Black regarded the books on the floor that had once been on the shelves, she did not merely see disarray. Rather, she saw at once order and the corruption of order. Each particle of what she perceived was an alloy of her commonsensical understanding of what she visually perceived—that is, a room in dishevelment, a fallen book, scattered papers—and its value laden opposite. Likewise, Mrs. Black did not simply see a "bad school," but she saw also a good school. In fact, she saw a good school that had adopted the pall of inferiority.

Mrs. Black proceeded to explain to me that the Department of Education (DOE) is very much a mirror image of the City of New York itself. According to her, there is a "big push" in the city to close public libraries and convert them into apartment buildings and condominiums. She summarized that the entire city is preoccupied with real estate as a primary money-making venture. Like the city, the DOE is getting rid of school libraries, she related. The reason that she was in The Academy was that the library at her former school had closed. At that time, she was "floating," meaning that she was affiliated with the book collection processes at different schools in New York City. She told me that although she was considered to be the school librarian, the school itself did not have a library. Instead, all the books were confined to one storage room, which doubled as her private administrative office. She offered to take me on a tour of that space.

I followed her down the main hallway; we turned left, down one of the windy, maze-like corridors. We made about three sharp turns before we arrived at our inconspicuous destination. It was a door without ceremony, non-official. She opened that door to what looked to me like a perpetual dusk. There was one light hanging perilously overhead, futilely attempting to breathe light into the innumerable blanknessess between the several stacks of books and clusters of paper. I could see the vestiges of attempts to organize the mess, yet ultimately, the mess persisted. Tall metal racks lined the room's perimeter, and some lingered inappropriately in the center. They were all filled with books of varying sizes and contents. Mrs. Black indicated that much of the material had been outdated due to a school budget that did not accommodate the purchase of current material. At one corner of the room was Mrs. Black's desk, which itself was buried under masses of books. There was a small corner near the front of the desk that contained some official-looking paperwork. Mrs. Black explained that some of these papers were book order forms. At a somewhat climactic moment during the tour, which involved only a modicum of spatial movement, Mrs. Black announced ironically, "This is our library."

If irony be the "discrepant engagement" (to borrow Nathaniel Mackey's neologism) of the actual and the expected, then the space of ironic articulation must reveal both in a single moment of utterance and in a single flash of apperception. The space of irony then would be the fourth dimension of apperception. The first through the third would be all the axes of phenomenal reality that compose the actual. The fourth would be the dimension-antithesis. In this room, then, there were gleaming shelves of books. The room was well-lit and populated with several antique-styled wooden tables (a suggestion of the lineage of scholastic pursuits to which all present learners were inevitably attached). Students sat here, busily completing homework assignments and research projects. Or, perhaps these students were just natural bibliophiles, reading at their leisure and pursuing various topics as a matter of sustained curiosity. Mrs. Black herself would be transformed into a real librarian, attending to a librarian's duties. Her desk would have inhabited its own office, separate from the general study area. This library and the office would both be separate from the storage area, which would contain all the most current editions of textbooks spanning from the staples of academic study (e.g., math, science, history, literature) to those associated with a more eclectic, nuanced vision of intellectual pursuits (i.e., Latin, Beginning Anthropology, Introduction to Philosophy).

From the bottom of the stairwell, through the gymnasium, down the compressed main passageway, which divided into two slim ducts, into the library-storage room was the diaphanous fourth dimension of irony. As suggested in the renderings of Jessica and Mrs. Black, those who lived within these four inseparable dimensions were subjected to the enactment of its unique set of "natural" laws. The inhabitants were not afforded the luxury of a dissociative consciousness, permitting them to reside within the most subtle of these dimensions. Neither could they attend, with hyper-parochiality, to the first three, with no awareness of the fourth. Because the materiality of their existence rested within the first three axes, the fourth was there to orient their psychical and emotional experiences in very particular ways. Both Jessica and Mrs. Black were quite aware that their individual and common domains were marked by states of utter abjection. Their perpetual experience of these spaces, therefore, was marked by dissatisfaction, disapproval, distaste, and displeasure.

Jessica and Mrs. Black had something else in common. Both suffered from forms of oppression. Re-evoking the insights of Gordon (2000), oppression is a circumstance in which people's life-options and capacity for self-assertion have been limited, a point that West corroborates, particularly regarding the character of institutional racism (1982). Jessica was oppressed in that she did not have the option of attending Randolph or another, more affluent, school of her choosing. As an African American student, her scholastic experience was the direct outcome of a racist symbolic order that bound her, relentlessly, to The Academy. A white woman, Mrs. Black experienced a different type of oppression, which may be classified as "professional." Professional circumstances had undermined her ability to choose a school of a caliber different from that of The Academy, and her ability to continue in the librarian career that she had initially chosen for herself. Yet, there is a fundamental difference between the oppression that Mrs. Black experienced and that Jessica lived within. Mrs. Black inhabited the ascendant arc of the symbolic order, had other professional options, some degree of social mobility, financial self-sufficiency, and the basic autonomy that is conferred to adulthood.

Jessica, by contrast, had none of these privileges. Jessica could either attend The Academy; drop out, thus ensuring a life of even greater degrees of personal and social immobility; or experience a more sinister end. In many ways, then, Jessica's field of possibilities resembles that of her pre-bellum ancestors, in which the only viable choices were chattel, pariah, or corpse. The plaintive lilt that colored her testimony, therefore, was the seasoned inflection of one who had chosen, among a paltry field of alternatives, to live within a Title I school. Like the grotesque and obscene lexicon of homo ludens in the Cameroonian postcolony (Mbembe 1992), and the melancholic intonations of the Africana subjects who incant from a place of "wounded kinship" (Mackey 1993), the texture of Jessica's voice in her complaint disclosed the "banality" of her condition.

Mrs. Black also had to choose her being in this predicament. Unlike Jessica, however, she had the resources of wisdom and experience to critically analyze her situation. She knew that she was a woman of somewhat limited possibilities, although she knew that she had far more than Jessica. Nevertheless, she was unhappy and discontented. One is left to wonder, then, what would be the outcome when Mrs. Black and the other faculty members at The Academy interface with Jessica and the other members of the latter's cohort? What would occur when the embodiments of banality, discontent, and abjection were forced to live with one another in one lightless environ? These questions will be the subject of the subsequent chapters. For now, in order to complete our exposition of the physical space of The Academy, it is worth expounding upon an example of an exception to the portrait that has been developing thus far.

Mr. Wheeler's classroom provided an antithesis to the general ironies that lurked beyond its territory. When I had initially visited his classroom, however, it was to some degree an extension of the general condition of the hallways. Many of the items for classroom use were in plastic bins, which were scattered around the room. Stacks of papers inhabited tables that were clustered in the center of the room. The students' desks outlined the room's perimeter. The general impression with which I was left was that the space was a work in progress. There were certainly elements of vibrancy in the midst. Colorful posters hung haphazardly along the walls. Many of these items, however, were in the bins and in various other stacks throughout the classroom.

Within one month, however, Mr. Wheeler's classroom had been completely reinvented. The walls no longer looked sullied and worn, but had been painted a gleaming, almost incandescent, white. The students' desks were no longer the content of the room's margins, but were centrally located. All learning material was now arranged neatly around the perimeter of the room. There were also various other items that created a sense of wonder to all who entered. A couple of formidable bookcases ran along one wall. On their shelves were all the wonders of the sciences: microscopes, telescopes, various artifacts, and jars containing amphibian brains submerged in formaldehyde. In one corner was a glass cage containing an entire ecosystem: a gerbil and a manmade forest.

Confirming the sense of wonder that the room inspired were four students who happened to wander in on a given day. They asked Mr. Wheeler if they could forego their recess period and stay in his room. Mr. Wheeler asked them why they wanted to do this. None of them could deliver a coherent answer. Following the general arc of their attention, Mr. Wheeler was able to glean that they wanted to stay in the room to play with the gerbil. He said to them: "If you want to stay in here to play with the gerbil, be straight with me. Is that what you want?" Somewhat bashfully, they acknowledged the correctness of his intuitions. They wended eagerly to the corner and began to engage the gerbil as if it were a pet, and simultaneously, as if it were a novel object of their collective curiosity. Many recess and lunch periods saw students inventing reasons to be inside Mr. Wheeler's room (which was probably due to a combination of the physical environment and Mr. Wheeler's engaging manner of relating to the students. The latter point will be addressed in a subsequent section).

Over the course of the nine months of fieldwork, I witnessed Mr. Wheeler's room continue to become more and more antithetical to the region just beyond it. By the end of the fourth month of the school year, his room had all new tables for student seating. All of them were a consistent white, becoming iridescent when fed by the light overhead. In return for the light, the tables projected back to the fixtures a luminescence of their own, and even radiated subtle, warm rays laterally and diagonally throughout the room. At each table was a small, clear container with pencils, calculators, protractors, and other science-related equipment. To the bookcases, which at first had been infused with a sense of wonder, were added an entire system of organization. There were several bins, each labeled with a different number, corresponding to a particular class of students. At the back of the room, positioned in relief to the freshly painted white walls, was a large, multicolored board consisting of science vocabulary words with their respective definitions. Underneath a large construction paper cutout of a capital "G" was the word "Gravity." "Acceleration" attended the "A" and "Inertia" occupied the space under the large "I."

By the end of the sixth month, the room had achieved yet another level of sophistication and elegance. All the tables were generally arranged around an epicenter, which was a larger table that consisted of newly purchased microscopes. The room now looked as if one would have been able to go there to conduct legitimate scientific research. Due to the manipulated effects of a new table arrangement, and the dynamic interplay of light and white paint, the room also appeared to have a lot more wide, open space. From the light fixtures now hung small laminated posters, each with a colorful montage illustrating a particular value. There was a poster for "Responsibility" and one for "Respect." Some posters contained entire maxims, such as "You are not finished when you lose. You are finished when you quit."

In the front of the room, there was a "Student of the Month" board. For each class, there were two black and white photographs. To the left of the entrance, there was a "Student Accomplishment" board, which was significantly larger than the "Student of the Month" board. The accomplishment board presented several examples of students' high scoring work.

If the first irony was constituted by the discrepant strata of phenomenal and fourth dimensionalities, Mr. Wheeler's classroom would be a region of the third that channeled the essence of the fourth. It could not have been a part of the fourth dimension, however, by virtue of its physical positioning in the phenomenal world. Mr. Wheeler's room was rather the space of the anomaly, the distraction, the diversion, the respite, the refuge, the special place, and the dream. What these students experienced in the pure physicality of Mr. Wheeler's room was not the rule, but rather the exception to their daily habitation of The Academy. There is a fundamental difference between the fourth dimensionality of Jessica's and Mrs. Black's experiences of the common areas and the library-storage room, and that of Mr. Wheeler's room. For Jessica and Mrs. Black, "other schools" were adumbrated in an infinite number of profound absences. In Mr. Wheeler's room, the fourth dimension had achieved a materiality in which the students were actively participating. The names and pictures on the walls belonged actually and indisputably to them. Their utilization of the microscopes, their adherence to the system of organization, their use of the bins, their handling of the learning materials, their intimate acquaintance with the gerbil and with the variegated accoutrements of science, were all a part of their lived experiences.

The physical transformations wrought in Mr. Wheeler's classroom and their correlation to the students' generally pleasant temperament are consistent with the results of Berry's research (2002). Furthermore, Mr. Wheeler's inscription of students' names and work upon the walls suggests the validity of Killeen's study, which concluded that putting students' work on the walls of classrooms gives children a sense of ownership of the space (2003). For students languishing under the weight of oppression, Mr. Wheeler's room restores a sense of transcendent possibilities. Perhaps the aptitudes that merited students a place on Mr. Wheeler's "Student of the Month" and "Student Accomplishment" boards were transferable to the outside world. Perhaps "Respect" would become more than just a laminated sign posted on the wall; perhaps respect would be what these children are one day able to command from their school, community, and the nation; it might even become a protocol with which they treat others. In short, a meaningful intervention into the spatio-temporal is simultaneously an intervention into the existential and the phenomenological, both contemporaneously and projectively—an instantiation of another resonant symbol.

The foregoing discussion concentrated on the ways that beings might be constituted intersubjectively, primarily between humans and built environments. In what follows the intersubjective field will pan outward to include exchanges between human subjects.

NOTES

1. Refer to the discussion of *symbolization* and *systemization* in chapter 1.
2. Refer also to the discussion of *resonation* in chapter 1.
3. This point is reminiscent of Urrieta's discussion of what he terms "assistentialism," which describes the practice of administering financial and social policies that merely address symptoms, rather than the root causes of social problems (2004). He describes NCLB as a classic assistentialistic law that does not address the root causes of the nation's persistent educational gap, but rather codes racial and ethnic minorities as intrinsically deficient. The cumulative effect of such legislation and policies is that the pedagogical subject is dehumanized, and reified as a degenerate social idiom. Urrieta proposes an "anti-assistentialistic" approach, which would humanize the pedagogical subject and encourage the input of families and community members to transform the educational edifice.

Chapter Four

The Bad School

The Academy had been labeled a "bad school" by all: teachers, administrators, students, the Department of Education, and the State of New York. The criteria determining this label, while overlapping among these different entities, was also very different depending upon one's vantage point. Many of the teachers and the administration felt that The Academy's deficiencies rested primarily in the various academic ineptitudes and behavioral indiscretions of the students. The gym teacher, Mrs. Price, a white woman in her mid-forties, offers one opinion of the overall quality of the school:

Me: "What are your impressions of the school?"

Mrs. Price: "This is a *bad school*. This school received an 'F' last year. It was really bad before. Fights all the time. . . ."

Me: "What else was going on in the school?"

Mrs. Price: "There was some really bad stuff happening at this school. This was the worst school in the city according to the grading system."

Mrs. Price's initial comment regarding the grade of the school indicates that her perception of the school was synonymous not only with what she had empirically observed since the previous year, but also with the pronouncements of the state. In fact, the state's grading system conferred an absolute identity upon the school: "F." This state-conferred identity subsequently informed how Mrs. Price perceived the school: The "worst school" in New York City.

Mrs. Black's insights mirror those held by Mrs. Price:

Me: "What are your impressions of the school?"

Mrs. Black, *motioning with her hands*: "Look around. This is a bad school. The kids do not know how to behave. The behavior is ingrained within the culture of the school."

Mrs. Black echoed Mrs. Price's blanket statement: "This is a bad school." Mrs. Price located the source of this badness within the students themselves. According to her, the students lacked fundamental knowledge of and ability for socially appropriate behavior, asserting that the students' transgressions were an integral feature of the school's culture.

Up to this point in the monograph, we have made copious mention of "the symbolic order" (or "symbolic systems"), that system of structured meanings and associations that permeates existence at various degrees of existential density, from the cognitive and emotional to the external and structural. We have also categorically defined the symbolic order in our present era to be inherently racist, hierarchical and dichotomous. If we arbitrarily assign a location to this "symbolic order"—let us say that it is "out there" (as opposed to occupying a space of interiority, which, as an act of metaphorical semiosis, would be equally valid)—then we might say that The Academy—as a physical, semiotic, legislative, and structure entity—is the centripetal instantiation of that order. This analogy is only meant to allow us to conceptualize how The Academy arrives into the world as a constituent of and promulgator of an extant order. I do not mean, however, to suggest that, as an instance of that order's centripetal vectors, The Academy does not undergo its own processes of semiosis. And indeed, both semioses must be accounted for in the explication of Mrs. Black's and Mrs. Price's comments.

In one respect, the imputing of degenerate cultural values to ethnic minorities and the spaces that they occupy is not inconsistent with larger cultural narratives about minorities. Educational research abounds that illustrates how white teachers tend to have lower and/or negative expectations of African American and other ethnic minority children (Winfield 1986; Marx 2008; Uhlenberg and Brown 2002). Muhammad Khalifa, for example, conducted a two-year ethnographic study that concluded that white teachers tended to assume that their African American students were intellectually and culturally inferior (2011). Yet the simultaneously epic and infinitesimal journey from the symbolic order to The Academy was mediated by those exercising governance over that institution. In assigning to The Academy a grade of "F" and deeming it the "worst school in the district," the New York City Department of Education infuses into The Academy a refurbished discourse of inferiority. Furthermore, a phenomenological reading of this discursive morphogenesis reveals how, for Mrs. Black and Mrs. Price, the

ascriptions "F" and "worst school" could achieve what appears to be nomothetic import.

In order for The Academy to have achieved a grade of "F," the Department of Education (DOE) had to collect various statistics with respect to
performance on math and English Language Arts (ELA) exams. Students'
performance on these tests was tabulated and measured against the performance of other students in the school system. In addition, The Academy's
current average scores for the math and ELA exams were compared with
their scores from the previous year. Compiled alongside such measurements
as "behavior," "attendance" and "academic merit," The Academy was then
given a "Progress" score (a numerical value) and a letter grade of "F" (criteria gathered from the New York City Department of Education [2011]).

Yet to refer to the "F" as an "ascription," as I have done erroneously up to
this point, is to miss its phenomenological value as a tropologically dense
region of experience. For, the "F" imports from the larger symbolic order the
purported veracity of conclusions arrived upon through scientific metrics. As
a legitimate conclusion, then, the "F" achieves momentum as an "in-itself,"
conceived in bad faith. Yet the bad faith of this claim to F-hood is not likely
to be punctured by those teachers who have recited to me this value-laden
edict of the Department of Education. Why? First, the moment in which they
uttered the DOE's truth, they restored their very own complicity with a
symbolic order that assumes (a) the truth of scientific measurements and (b)
the inherent inferiority of ethnic minorities. All the "F" must do to conceal its
own inherently mercurial activity is to "encapsulate" (in Clarke's parlance)
the larger narratives of historically constituted social inequities. Trouillot is
particularly instructive here, as he reasons that labels are nothing more than
neat metaphorical conceits that mask histories of dehumanization (1995,
2003). Sara Ahmed makes a similar point regarding the ways in which the
rhetoric surrounding diversity is an instance of "non-performativity," and
paradoxically, precluding real acts of inclusion (2012).

Earlier I discussed bad faith and good faith as kinetically and mutually
constitutive, rather than static positions distributed between two poles. And
indeed, the being of The Academy as an "F" and as "a bad school" is the
result of this same kinetic procedure. However, the kinesis here, wrought
through the machinations of semiosis, scientism, edict and the sovereign rule
of the New York City Department of Education, achieves nomothetic inertia.

Evidence of this inertia is embedded in Mr. Wheeler's and the other
faculty members' divergent readings of an incident with one particular student. Mr. Wheeler, who is of African American and Puerto Rican descent,
explained to me that one African American male student, Andy, "single-
handedly put The Academy on the map," due to several instances of sexual
harassment. Apparently, Andy was facing several criminal charges as a result
of his actions. Mr. Wheeler continued, explaining that "cultural differences

are partly to blame for the charges." The "teachers thought his comments were inappropriate, when they [comments] were just the result of his culture." Mr. Wheeler also indicated that such misreading was endemic to the culture of the school. According to him, what the students perceived as socially appropriate was different from what the school faculty members deemed as proper ways of behaving and communicating.

Many of the teachers' opinions of the school and its student population did not allow for the compassionate reading exemplified by Mr. Wheeler's comments. Both for Mrs. Black and Mrs. Price, the school was "bad" and the students were undisciplined and offensive. According to two other teachers, Mrs. Beal, a white woman, and Mr. Anderson, a white man, the students were "challenging." Of the eight lead teachers who were asked to express their opinions about the school and its students, four (all white) offered perspectives that could be characterized as negative.

The discrepancy between Mr. Wheeler's analysis of the school and that of his colleagues warrants further explanation. Irvine (1990) corroborates Mr. Wheeler's analysis of Andy's imminent suspension. She indicates that because white teachers fail to comprehend the culture of African American students, the former tend to misinterpret and denigrate the latter's manners of communication, non-verbal gestures, learning styles and worldviews. The cumulative result is that white teachers tend to have negative opinions of black students' culture (Ladson-Billings 1995). Khalifa discovered, by contrast, that because black teachers tend to be culturally in sync with black students, these teachers tend to affirm their black students and can inspire greater academic achievement (2011).

We must be careful not to assume, however, that the disparity between what white and black teachers tend to achieve with black students is a consequence of simplistic assumptions about the nature of identification and misrecognition (i.e., like recognizes like, different misrecognizes different). The explanation is much more complex. In a compelling study based on forty-four oral history interviews with teachers in the coastal plains of North Carolina, Hilton Kelly demonstrated how even in under-resourced schools in the Jim Crow South, black schoolteachers who had previously taught in segregated schools, and black teachers in present-day disadvantaged schools were able to motivate and inspire disadvantaged children to achieve the means of educational and social capital (2010). Furthermore, many of these teachers came into the pedagogical setting with distinct philosophies of racial uplift that stood in critique to white supremacy. True, these teachers were compelled by an emic comprehension of the plight of their charges; however, this identification does not discount the fact that the effectiveness of the teachers was predicated upon a lived and demonstrated desire to see their students advance in all areas of life. Intervening into the very symbolic order that has philosophically deduced the inferiority of black subjects, then, these teachers engage in a pedagogical revolution discussed in various ways by Woodson (1933), Du Bois (1903), and Freire (1970).

If the white teachers at The Academy had already conferred the pall of inferiority onto their black students, and enacted their pedagogical rituals with a religiosity supported by the sacred texts of racist mythologies, centripetally kinetic symbolic orderings of meaning, and the Department of Education statistical metrics (the pious descendent of phrenology), how then could these same teachers feel a sense of social responsibility to their black students comparable to that of a Mr. Wheeler? And, in not feeling this social responsibility, these acolytes of "the bad school" simultaneously affirmed its sanctity (or would it be profanity?) and deny their own role in its continual restitution. "Deny" here is the operative concept, as it represents the anachronistic character of bad faith kinetics. In disavowing the ontogenetic relation between the racial system of oppression and the current predicament of racial minorities in "bad schools," these teachers at once assign the tropological density of "inferiority" a priori to the students; and sacrosanctity, purity, blamelessness to their whiteness and to their total beings. The restitution, therefore, is of the very same dichotomous hierarchy of racial oppression mentioned earlier.

Mrs. Coby, a white woman in her mid-sixties, offered a more probing analysis of the problems that the school had with the students. Having been an educator for approximately twenty years, and having worked in a number of different capacities in New York Public Schools (teaching, administration, and others), she had a broad perspective on the entire matrix of public education in New York City:

Mrs. Coby: "Nobody wants them. [*She repeats.*] Nobody wants them."

Me: "Is there some sort of selection process for middle school?"

Mrs. Coby, *nodding earnestly*: "There is. Principals look at the profiles of prospective students and say, 'I want this one; I don't want this one.'"

Mrs. Coby *continues, switching topics somewhat*: "I took my own children out of public school and put them into Catholic school. . . . Neither Klein [New York City Public School System Superintendent] nor Bloomberg's [New York City Mayor at that time] children are in public school. All of their children are in private school. They won't even put their children in public school!"

According to Mrs. Coby, students are either chosen to attend or denied access to particular schools based on their academic and behavioral profiles. Many of the attendees at The Academy were students who had been rejected by other middle schools. Upon their very entry into the school, then, they were pronounced undesired and discarded. They were the residue of an edifice that has ambitions of commendable functioning. They were left over from a process of trimming and refining something into a particular image of ideality.

In the making of this ideality, what happens to those who are trimmed away, excised? From the moment of their extraction, they are cast as incommensurable with the material of ideality. Or rather, they become the denizens of the nether region of a four-dimensional irony. The production of the ideality and the non-ideality for that matter may be thought of as the unfolding of a psychoanalytic procedure already in progress. We must recall Manganyi here (1981), who would align whiteness with the ideality and blackness with the non-ideality. For, in having already relegated this predominantly black and Latina(o) population to the nadir of our prevailing symbolic order, the excision from the student bodies of other schools in the district would be the logical next step, the structural fulfillment of what had already occurred in the semiotic realm.

The difficulty of placing these discarded souls echoes what Du Bois defined as a central problematic for our country during the post-bellum period (1903). According to Du Bois, during the post-emancipation era the nation was baffled as to what it should do with the thousands of newly manumitted black people who populated the American South. The crux of the matter was essentially how the nation was going to effectively integrate this black plenum—whom the nation had been so relentless in making into creatures of animalistic servility—effectively into the social and economic fabric of the country. And, despite the ambitious, yet utterly ineffectual, efforts of the Freedman's Bureau, that integration never occurred. It never occurred semiotically and it certainly did not occur structurally. More than one hundred years later, the nation is still trying to determine what to do with this plenum—one that is no longer just black, but more ethnically and linguistically diverse. And, like the Freedman's Bureau, the No Child Left Behind legislation and its attendant systems—high-stakes testing, school rankings, funding imperatives, and admissions standards—have proven ineffectual.

Once these students assume the cloak of the ironic, and of non-ideality, what then is the arc, where lay the limit of their movements through the realms of public perception, the educational edifice and the larger social matrix? Can any semblance of ideality be achieved by the student who has already been marked as the antithesis of the ideal? Will the students think that ideality is an option for their future realities? In other words, how do these particular accretions of symbols resonate personally, intersubjectively and socioculturally? The answers to these questions are suggested by the testimonies of the students themselves.

One Puerto Rican student, Lydia, offers her opinion of The Academy:

Lydia: "What are you doing?"

Me: "I am here to do research on your school."

Lydia: "So, you do research on bad schools?"

Me: "This is not the point of my research."

Lydia: "This is a bad school!?"

On a separate occasion, a second individual, an African American student named Harry, corroborates Lydia's statement. He maintains a proverbial ironic grin and sarcastic inflection in his voice as he and I converse about his opinions of the school. He begins by asking me what I'm writing. I answer:

"Notes about the classroom."

Harry: "I thought you were writing good stuff."

Me: "It's neither good nor bad—just what I see."

Harry: "What are you writing it for?"

Me: "I am doing a research project about New York Public Schools."

Harry, *in comic disbelief*: "You're writing about this school?"

Me: "Do you like this school?"

Harry, *as if the answer is obvious, making facial gestures of disgust*: "No."

Me: "Why?"

Harry: "There are black people here."

Me: "I think I misheard you; what did you say?"

Harry, *with a laugh*: "There are bad people here."

Me: "There are bad people here?"

Harry: "You don't hear them."

*At that moment in our conversation, a boy serendipitously leaned over to Harry and whispered in his ear: "Suck my ****."*

What is interesting here is that the vocabulary used by the teachers ("bad school") was consonant with how both of my younger interviewees framed their perceptions. Harry's particular objection was with the students themselves. For him, the truth of his assessment was self-evident. With the classic banality and ironic humor of one who has assumed the being of homo ludens,[1] Henry entreated me to look and listen in order to verify what he had said. Yet, behavior was only one part of the empirically verifiable truth of the school's badness. Harry's "truth" was distinctly racial. For him, the source of the school's non-ideality rested in the presence of black people. His embarrassed substitution of "black" for "bad" suggests also a perceived equivalency between the two ideas. Because the student himself was also black, I am curious about his perception of himself. Did the boy perceive himself as bad? Was he a non-ideality to himself? As a matter of syllogistic course, it would naturally follow that he did indeed perceive himself as a "bad" individual.

Yet, how could he formulate a different notion? The Academy was nothing more than an extension of a more encompassing symbolic order, one that had already assigned him and his classmates to an inferior position within that order, one that was perennially restored in the attitudes of the teachers and the administrators, and one that had the weight of scientific metrics to confirm its validity.

Lydia and other students presented additional meanings entailed in the idea of The Academy as a "bad school." During the course of my previously cited conversation with Lydia, I asked:

"What makes it [The Academy] bad?"

Lydia: "The teachers don't care. There are a lot of fights. Mr. Wheeler cares though!"

Me: "How do you know when a teacher doesn't care?"

Lydia: "They don't give you homework. They let you get away with anything. They let you be bad and never say nothing."

Like the teachers with whom I conversed, Lydia held the blanket opinion that the school was "bad" and the students were behaviorally challenged. Unlike the teachers, however, who consistently asserted that the school's difficulties were primarily a function of various student inadequacies, Lydia attributed The Academy's difficulties to both the students and the teachers. To the blanket judgment of the school as "bad," Lydia added another: "The teachers don't care."

Another student on a separate occasion corroborated Lydia's judgment that the teachers were uncaring. She and I had a conversation about her English teacher, Mrs. Beal, a white woman in her early forties:

Crystal: "I don't like her!"

Me: "Why don't you like her?"

Crystal: "She doesn't teach. We learned about metaphors and similes the day before the [state] test. She didn't really teach us. For another assignment, we had to memorize the names of stars and write them down. [*She exclaimed rhetorically about the assignment.*] What is that!?"

For both Lydia and Crystal, this lack of care was directly related to the fact that the teachers were not committed to assigning homework and rigorous classwork, and enforcing standards of discipline. The uncaring disposition is perfectly consistent with how an individual would feel about something that he or she has deemed "disposable," "bad," and "inferior." (I would imagine too that teachers' detachment from their students may be exacerbated by the detachment that they would feel within an aesthetically unkempt, uncared-for environment—see chapter 3.) The daily rite of not assigning homework kinetically infuses the students' phenomenological experience of The Academy with these tropological densities. Daily, the students must experience their own conferred disposability, inferiority, and badness, and must choose how they will live within this tropological field.

More often than not, I found students choosing to live within their circumstances critically, ironically, and with hostility. Implicit in Lydia's comments and even more resonant in Crystal's was a desire for an ideality that was thwarted, consumed by the general predicament. Although Lydia acknowledged that the majority of the teachers at The Academy did not care, as evident in the lack of rigor of the work assigned, she privileged a standard that was essentially different from the one to which she was daily subjected. There was no equability between the prevailing predicament and the particular standard that she acknowledged as the more desirable one. What was taken as a cardinal virtue was not extant within the walls of The Academy. The virtue itself had to be imported from elsewhere, then used to measure the value of the situation at hand. Like Lydia, Crystal privileged a standard opposite the one she daily encountered. Crystal, however, did not simply express her disdain for the situation; she went further to assume that Mrs. Beal's norms of engaging the students warranted an ad hominem attack. Crystal took the teacher's practices as personal assaults and responded with feelings of dislike. I witnessed on one occasion Crystal giving form to her dislike by cursing angrily at Mrs. Beal.

Andy, the student who, by acquiring sexual harassment charges, "single-handedly" put The Academy "on the map," expressed a similar hostility toward his math teacher:

Me: "Do you like math?"

Andy: "No."

Me: "Why?"

Andy: "I don't like the teacher."

Me: "Why?"

Andy: "She be talkin' about people's mother; she be sayin' crazy stuff."

Me: "She talks about your mother?"

Andy: "No! She know better. My mother don't like her and she would come up here and beat the shit outta her."

Andy's disdain for his math teacher, an African American woman in her mid-forties, has a two-part phenomenological structure. The first part is cognitive, a function of the polymous symbol, the bad school. The second part, however, the affective, is the epiphenomenal residue of living within the symbolic constellation of the bad school and within an overall state of oppression. Additionally, the affective dimension of Andy's disdain is essentially a moral judgment,[2] a criticism of the sacrilegious practice of publicly insulting one's mother. Again, such sacrilege is not inconsistent with the behavior of one who has already deemed The Academy's students as disposable and inferior.

Within Crystal's, Lydia's, and Harry's pronouncements of the school as bad, and Crystal's and Andy's demonstrations of anger, there was an entire critique of the scholastic environment and a proposal for solutions. All three students were insisting upon a social and academic ideal to which they, at that time, had no access.

Andy proceeded to make a direct connection between his English curriculum and his future possibilities.

Me: "Do you like English?"

Andy simply looked at me with hostile seriousness, and shook his head.

Me: "Why?"

Andy: "She [Mrs. Beal] don't give challenging work."

Me: "What kind of work does she give you?"

Andy: "Baby work. It's not gonna get me nowhere."

All of my interviewees agreed that the work that the teachers assigned at The Academy, particularly that which Mrs. Beal assigned, was evidence that the teachers did not "care" and valued students negatively. Andy, however, went a step further to acknowledge that his English curriculum would circumscribe his possibilities in life. What all the students experienced and to which they bore witness on a daily basis, and what Andy so wisely articulated, was their common state of potential-limiting oppression. Despite the fact that the predominant disposition of the students, at least in their interviews, was not ludic (with the exception of Harry), Mbembe would certainly consider their discourses of complaint and hostility to have emerged from the discrepant space between their aspirations to a humanizing ideality and the unalterable condition of a veritable *commandment*.

We are now in a position to reinterpret Crystal's outbursts, Andy's hostility and his imminent expulsion, Harry's egregious race logic, Lydia's negative judgments of the school, and the teachers' comments that The Academy consisted of students who were "challenging." These students were not morally and culturally degenerate, as they had very well-defined standards of rectitude and justice. These students were in effect offering, in their genuflections, a critical commentary on their oppressed predicament. Undergirding this commentary was a preoccupation with an ideality of a future that might disclose itself as a real possibility. The students' perpetual complaint echoes Lewis's argument that questions of utopia are inextricably linked to education and educational critical theory (2006). This idea also runs parallel to Levine's (1978), Webber's (1978), and Henry's (2000) insight that black slaves were always projecting themselves toward a more propitious future. What is represented in Lewis's utopic vision for education—pedagogical praxis that does not succumb to the deadening rituals attending a high-stakes testing regime in the late capitalist era (2010)—and in Du Bois's specific prescriptions in *Darkwater* for a society languishing under the oppressive weight of capitalism (1920), is that "utopic" longings or aspirations toward a future "good" in subaltern studies are primarily defined by a fundamental insistence upon humanization. In other words, utopian philosophies that concern peoples living within oppressive circumstances tend to have a fundamental point of commonality: the desire to be treated as human beings (see also Halpin [2003] and Jameson [2004]).

The Academy had been constituted as a dystopic space; it was a "failing" school and the diametrical antithesis of an ideal place in which to educate children. Within this dystopia, the various elements of the tropological field—discarded, uncared for, challenging (which is nothing more than a euphemism for an exceedingly more pejorative sentiment), morally and culturally degenerate, inferior, black, dim social prospects—are but refractions of a single, more elemental tropological density: "bad." For, in our symbolic order, "bad" is the most fundamental position of the nethermost, descendent arc. These children, therefore, were "living" within the nadir of a symbolic, social and pedagogical order, one that undermined their very humanity. And, their souls chose to live—through affective comportment, the pre-objective and objective adoption of particular symbolic networks—within this order in various modes of utopic discontent: critical, ludic, angry, and ironic. In their laughter, tirades, sporadic entrances and exits, they were engaging in a type of, what Jafari Allen calls, "political insurgence," in which "those small acts" serve the function of "rehumanizing in the midst of dehumanizing" (2011: 84).

And yet, when attempting to understand the phenomenological experiences of the students at The Academy, I cannot help but be confronted with a region of interminable inaccessibility. Daily, these students attended a "bad school," perpetually dealt with "bad students," were under the supervision of "bad teachers" who "do not care," and were required to do things that would not help them "go" anywhere in life. Although I bore intimate witness to their reality and was able to intellectually extract particles of their experience, I did not have to "live" inside of this phenomenological terrain. I did not share their particular experience of being "unwanted" or of having my possibilities circumscribed in the same ways. Triangulating the vantage points from which I observed these realities, and diversifying the objects in my fields of perception allowed me to at least approach a center that would remain inexorably unreached.

In this chapter I have tried primarily to understand how students came to be in their existential confrontation with what Geertz would call the "polysemous" or poly-accretive trope of "the bad school." I relied primarily on students' and, to a lesser extent, teachers' accounts of their experiences within The Academy. The following chapter shifts the focus more acutely toward the constitution of the teachers' beings and the intersubjective play of those beings with students' beings. What immediately follows will rely on interviews of teachers and students, and third-party observation.

NOTES

1. Refer to the discussion in chapter 1 of Mbembe and *homo ludens.*
2. Refer to the chapter 1 discussion of Goluboff, who argues that particular affective structures are value judgments (2011).

Chapter Five

Androids and Infernal Feedback Loops

When recording my observations of the teachers at The Academy, I encountered a particularly formidable challenge to the methodological goal of rigorous intuition. Many of them exhibited a quality that I had a difficult time pinning down in precise, classificatory terms. I suppose that, although I was easily able to acknowledge that neither the being nor the substance of the experiences of the students could ever be accessed, I did not think that other elements of the milieu would be equally as elusive. As I watched and listened to the teachers, one simple descriptor continued to present itself as my prevailing impression of them: "weakness." While there were empirically observable traits and behaviors commensurate with this impression, the impression itself always felt like something more than the sum of these; it was something felt and intuited (and to be certain, a part of my impression even was derived from the inaccessible depths of my own subjective imaginings). The teachers appeared weak, meager, lifeless, without verve, worn, tattered, bored, and absent. Eyes, nervous and unsteadied, vacant and course-less, were enclosed by the dark circles of age and worry. The character of their gaze was not unlike what I have encountered while observing people classified as mentally ill. The difference was that these teachers at least had all the accoutrements of functionality and normalcy. The shells of them, with the efficiency of an android, went about their daily routines. Yet, each of these androids, at his or her core, was essentially vacant. It was as if they had never even been in possession of the thing that is supposed to take residence in the void region of human interiority. There had been no fire that simply diminished to a warm glow. There appeared to be an immemorial and utter vacuity.

There was a similar vacancy in their voices. On many occasions in the fieldnotes, I noted a freakish inaudibility in their manner of speaking. Three teachers in particular would frequently talk to students, administering directives, retributions, and instructions, yet I would have to strain to hear what they said. I almost got the impression that the import of their words, and even the compelling force (whether insight or emotion) that infuses the urgency of a particular utterance, was simply non-existent, or too feebly constituted to have a real impact.

Their bodily movements and gesticulations were equally enervated. They moved slowly, without urgency, without dispatch. I would often find them feebly standing, humped over an assemblage of papers clasped in their hands, as they walked or spoke to students. Their eyes rarely left their stacks. They were dependent on these papers for an anchor, or perhaps as a makeshift barrier between themselves and the students. In the ethnographic record, I encountered seemingly unquantifiable instances of teachers exhibiting "weakness" in one form or another in their exchanges with students.

Mrs. Black illustrates this point well. On one particular day, Mr. Wheeler was running a little late to his science class. In his stead, Mrs. Black supervised his students. Although she was a substitute for this particular class period, she was a permanent fixture in the school and quite familiar to all the students. She walked into the class, and without acknowledging the students, simply wrote on the board: "Mr. Wheeler will be a little late. He said to review your homework." Students continued to engage in private conversations after she had written the instructions. No one regarded the board. After about five minutes, she erased the second sentence, replacing it with another: "He said to take a science book from the class library." A girl ate a breakfast sandwich from a deli. Another student ate a deli sandwich and a bag of Cheetos. From observing Mr. Wheeler's class previously, I knew that eating while class was in session was prohibited. For about ten minutes, Mrs. Black did not verbally communicate with the students at all. The directives that she wrote on the board were not reinforced by direct communication with the students.

The vacuum created by Mrs. Black's verbal abstinence was a breeding ground for the whimsies of sixth, seventh, and eighth graders. One boy began to beat on his desk, making very intricate polyrhythms. While an obvious expression of musical virtuosity, this behavior was generally not allowed during normal class time. Mrs. Black placed her hand timidly on the boy's shoulder and whispered as she pointed to me, "We are not alone; there is a researcher in the room." This boy ceased, yet others had taken their cue from his initial brazenness. Various iterations of noise and music erupted around the room. One boy beat a table loudly with a plastic bottle. Others were engaged in boisterous jokes, tirades, and various other exchanges. Mrs. Black tried to address all of these instances, timidly touching shoulders. She was not even remotely successful with any of them. There were just too many holes that needed to be plugged, and they seemed to be multiplying exponentially.

One boy spun a basketball on his finger and lost control of it repeatedly. Mrs. Black, who was standing close by, uttered an almost inaudible, "Stop," yet for the duration of the boy's self-amusement, she was silent. At one point the ball almost hit her. She finally asked the boy to relinquish the basketball to her control. Her command could barely be heard. The boy refused. She continued to ask for the ball, but the boy repeatedly denied her. At one point, she even reached for the ball, also unsuccessfully. He finally placed the object on the floor between his own chair and that of another student; it was out of her reach. He kept his left hand on it to secure its inaccessibility. Mrs. Black finally capitulated without having acquired the ball. She softly told him to "stop playing with the ball," as she departed from him.

Silently, Mrs. Black proceeded to the classroom "library," which consisted of a couple of shelves of books, retrieved several paperbacks and began distributing them to individual tables, each consisting of three to five students. Her actions were not accompanied by speech. None of the students truly engaged the texts. Some of them flipped through briefly, commenting casually upon the pictures. At one table of girls I saw books entitled *Wild Babies* and *A Wood Frog's Life*. At a table of boys I saw two others: *Building or Ice House* and *The Channel: The Building of a 200-Year Old Dream*. There was another book about construction, entitled *Demolition*. All these books were thin paperbacks that looked as if they belonged in an elementary school.

The students quickly ignored these mere parodies of intellection and the entire room devolved into randomness. Sporadic outbursts occurred, and students left the room and returned at will. Mrs. Black offered a weak "Shhhh" occasionally, but this gesture was not honored. Eventually, she became a passive spectator to all that transpired around her. She looked disturbed, with a hint of criticism twisting the corners of her eyebrows. Occasionally, she made a feeble attempt to reprimand a student. At that point, however, I was not sure that these reprimands were subtended by any expectations at all. Mrs. Beal eventually entered the doorway, spoke something inaudibly, and gently motioned for the students to go with her. They all grabbed their belongings, and, without ceremony, exited, leaving the room in utter disarray.

We must be reminded here that for Mrs. Black, "bad school" had already been the tropological substance of her habitation of The Academy. Furthermore, she had already conferred upon the students the tropological density of "not knowing how to behave" (refer to chapter 4). The students also had conferred upon themselves the tropological being of "bad students," upon the school the being of "a bad school," and upon Mrs. Black the being of "a bad teacher." And, as we established in the previous chapter, if the "bad school" had already reached its densest tropological point, achieved in-itselfness through scientistic modes of validation and through a symbolic order that ritually regenerates itself on a daily basis, then, on that day, for the students to become "bad students" and Mrs. Black to become a "bad teacher" was practically inevitable.

On the students' parts, it was virtually impossible for them to choose to be anything other than the options that were presented to them in that moment. They certainly could not achieve a being consonant with the domain of ideality. Among the options remaining, they had the conferred being of the "bad student/challenging student/culturally and morally vacant," which Mrs. Black actively championed (although a Pyrrhic victory at best), sustained, and instilled through her relative passivity and withdrawal. The students could have inserted themselves into the hiatus between this first designation and the iconoclast—what we referred to earlier as a disposition of utopic discontent, positioning themselves critically, ludically, angrily, or passively within the total situation. However, based solely on outward behavior, it probably would be very difficult to distinguish between those who had chosen to be "bad" and those who acted out of utopic aspirations. (In fact, there is an ample body of research that suggests that students' various forms of withdrawal from the pedagogical setting are in reality rejections of racial discrimination [Felice 1981], and an academic curriculum that has no direct connection to their experiences [Ladson-Billings 1995].) The "iconoclast" in this instance is nothing more than a theoretical placeholder, an asymptotic limit that was not impossible, yet highly improbable. For, the iconoclast would have the clarity, and the social and communicative resources to oppose the total structure directly, rather than through passionate genuflection.

Furthermore, to offer a cliché understatement that is comical because of its simultaneous simplicity and explanatory merit: Mrs. Black did not really *help* the situation. From her downcast gaze, to the full run of her affective trajectory from timorousness to an androidal withdrawal, she reiterated her concurrence with the symbolic order and the DOE's calculations. In fact, she became an avatar of, a prefect for, that order's ideals and pronouncements. In her dissociative engagements with the students, Mrs. Black adhered to the same anachronistic logic of bad faith—unwittingly she was creating the very situation (beings and behaviors) against which she dared to position herself as a meek, harmless victim.

If we establish a point of intersection between Sartre, Manganyi, and Hooks, then Mrs. Black's withdrawal and her victimhood may be read as an indulgence in a particular type of racial fantasy. In my own reading of Sartre in chapter 1, I established that bad faith and good faith are kinetic features of consciousness, moving about as a part of a single circadian motion. The bad faith of whiteness, for instance, is doomed to repeat a cycle whereby the changeability of that whiteness would be acknowledged and perpetually disavowed. Manganyi suggests that whiteness is a capacious existential reality that composes itself from all that is deemed "good." He further argues that in order to constitute itself as white/good, then it must disavow all that is "bad." The disavowed material becomes the equally capacious existential trope, "blackness." Through Fanon, Hooks maintains that whiteness "envies" those parts of its own being (among which are the body, sexuality, and moral degeneracy) that, in bad faith, it chooses to deny and displace onto a black alterity. This envy accounts for whiteness's occasional indulgence in black alterity, which resides at once within the very interior of whiteness and in the exteriorization of that interior, blackness. Such envy would account for whiteness's frivolous peregrinations on the grounds of black music, black fashion, black communicative styles, and black bodies, before taking refuge in the metastable region of contrived white providentiality. Due to the schismatic and schizophrenic topography of whiteness—consisting of a blackness (e.g., body, pleasure, fun, amorality) that is topographically there, yet not supposed to be there—it would make sense that these excursions would be characterized by emotional and cognitive dissociation.

Mrs. Black's assumption of victimhood, therefore, which properly belongs to the black region of her white being, can be nothing more than an exhilarating sojourn into a forbidden territory. Having already constituted the pedagogical and racial other as object, human-antithesis, acted upon, for the span of forty-five minutes, she pretended that she was all of these things before she eventually resurged into the realm of options, rights, and privileges. Yet, from the standpoint of the students Mrs. Black was, by far, not the most detestable creature in their midst.

Judging from innumerable comments that I overheard, either in the form of irascible soliloquies or in exchanges between peers, and from unquantifiable facial and bodily choreographies, Mrs. Beal, the English teacher, was by far the most hated teacher, and arguably, individual, in The Academy. And coincidentally, she was the prototype for the vacancy that I saw in the faces and heard in the utterances of the majority of teachers on campus. During one particular day that I entered her room, I found the students creating one of their usual spectacles of chaos. They were yelling all sorts of creatively spun obscenities, and departing and reemerging at will. She asked, her voice faint and aloof, for them to return to their seats, all the while languidly rotating her wrist toward herself, with a hollow, elliptical flutter of the hand. Neither her words nor her gestures produced the desired response. The one reaction that she did receive was an irreverent outburst from a male student, Curtis: "I don't like you because you are mean!" I found an opportune moment to discreetly ask him what prompted his outburst:

Me: "Why don't you like Mrs. Beal?"

Curtis: "She don't teach us nothing. This is the first time that she has taught us all year."

Me: "So what does she normally do?"

Curtis: "Sit at her desk and read a book." [*He looks at me with an expression teetering between indignant certitude and suggestive accusation.*]

As class progressed, Mrs. Beal attempted to present a lesson on the American Revolution (I learned that Mrs. Beal also teaches history). Her voice was not loud enough to be heard even by someone sitting close to her. The presentation was met with frequent interruptions. Or rather, the general din of the class was the prevailing activity, which was periodically interrupted by moments of futile instruction. Competing with the private interchanges of the students, Mrs. Beal would address particular behaviors. The subjects of the reprimands would respond with curses and threats.

Curtis's, like that of my other student interviewees, was a righteous indignation, filled with critical commentary on his situation and his teacher. And, like Mrs. Black, Mrs. Beal, through her daily enacted weakness, created the very situation in which she was immersed. Mrs. Beal's withdrawal was much more kinetically charged and was conducted with much more of the fervor of religiosity than Mrs. Black's, however. The book-wall that she, according to Curtis's testimony (a testimony that is corroborated by my own ethnographic observations), erected between herself and the students on a daily basis, consummated the ontological closure of the "bad, disposable student" to which her charges directed their utopic contestations. Furthermore, the brashness of such a gesture makes it a histrionic restaging (and unfolding) of the very historical drama that created this moment.

Mrs. Beal's brazenness recalls the observations of Nathan Haymes, who suggests that for the slave, the acquisition of literacy was inextricably linked to a project of humanization. Thus, the withholding of literacy from the slave was a deliberate act of dehumanization, a perpetual act of diminishing the slave to the status of an animal and an object (2001). Mrs. Beal, an English teacher, invested with the responsibility of ensuring that students achieve literacy and English language proficiency (it must be kept in mind also that these students, according to the State of New York, already had significant challenges with literacy) erected her wall, imperiously laying claim to literacy and depriving her pupils of this very spoil. The flagrance of such a gesture was certainly not lost on Curtis and, most likely, his classmates.

On the day in question, the general tone of hostility and irreverence was so evident that for me to engage Mrs. Beal in a conversation about her relationship with the students was an organic result of my presence in her room. Unprompted, Mrs. Beal began to relate to me her feelings about the school and the students:

> "This isn't the type of school I'm used to. I am not used to this. I was a literacy coach. I just got back into the classroom. Prior to coming here I worked in Special Ed. I don't know why they give me such anger. I don't know why they give me such anger [*she repeated*]. They do not like me. I used to give challenging work, but it was too hard for them, so I toned it down. Mr. Wheeler gives easier work to them, which builds confidence. I would like to give harder work, but they can't handle it. I don't know why they behave for Mr. Wheeler, but not for me. These kids are challenging. Last year they were on lockdown and couldn't leave their classrooms. There could be no traffic in the hallways."

One notable point of interest in Mrs. Beal's complaint was that, immediately following her "bafflement" as to why students did not like her, she commented upon the fact that she no longer gave challenging work. Had I been a little more astute in the moment I would have asked her if she thought that there was a direct correlation between the work that she gave and the students' attitudes toward her. Although I cannot state definitively whether or not she was aware that this particular correlation did exist, the consecutive nature of the two statements in question would seem to suggest that she was indeed cognizant of this connection. If we assume that she was cognizant, then her expression of disbelief was disingenuous. Perhaps her utterances were meant to mask embarrassment and the personally held conviction that she was practicing something that was essentially objectionable, especially given the fact that she would spend a great deal of her time reading for leisure during class. Like Mrs. Black, Mrs. Beal is indulging, in bad faith masochism, in the fantasy of victimhood.

Her hallucinogenic flight into this virtual fantasy was complete. In fidelity to the part that she was playing, she had internalized an identity (not merely a dramatic persona) as a powerless and disliked teacher. In her reprimands of the students, in her teaching of the curriculum, therefore, I beheld prescience. She knew that she would be met with hostility and resistance. The fact of students not liking her was a part of her ongoing awareness every time she interacted with them. She had essentially become their judgments of her. She was irremediably disliked, vacant, weak, inaudible, and ineffective, yet, to borrow Sartre's terminology, fundamentally "inauthentic."

Another notable issue that emerges from Mrs. Beal's comments is that she cast the students as behaviorally and intellectually "challenged." These judgments and her admission that she gave less challenging work appear consistent with Crystal's, Curtis's, and Andy's objections to her and what they perceived to be her insultingly simplistic curriculum.

That the students were intellectually inept was a prevailing attitude among the teachers in The Academy. For instance, when I asked Ms. Rector, a white teacher of about forty years old, her impressions of the students, she began speaking with all the ginger and tact that she could muster: "And the kids here are . . . " she then paused and leaned in toward me, " . . . border-line." She proceeded to qualify her words with a pleading expression, an extended arm, and an incessant swivel of her right wrist; then again she paused, before she finally stated in a pointless attempt to temper the gravity of her words; "borderline intelligence."

Mrs. Beal's, Mrs. Black's, and Ms. Rector's comments are consonant with the abundant research on how low teacher expectations of minority students' intellectual abilities and behavioral aptitudes have adverse consequences for student achievement (Jussim 1989; Brophy 1983; Jussim and Eccles 1992; Rubie-Davies 2006). These perceptions tend to be more informed by the teachers' own preconceptions than any real evidence from the students themselves (Uhlenberg and Brown 2002; Rong 1996; Cooper 2003). It is also not coincidental that overwhelmingly, teachers arrive into the classroom with lower expectations for black and Latina(o) students than for white students (McKown and Weinstein 2008). Because of these pejorative judgments of black and Latina(o) students, teachers are more likely to lower their expectations, "make deals" with students and "dumb down" the curriculum (Khalifa 2011; Rong 1996; Lightfoot 1978).

In this dumbing down, then, we behold another instance of oppression. For, it has been a running premise up to this point that one can only make a choice of himself or herself amid the various possibilities available in a particular socio-historical moment. For these students, if high expectations are perpetually withheld, and teachers are playing at being victims rather than making meaningful contributions to the pedagogical environment, then the choice of a purposeful, engaging, productive educational experience is foreclosed. Like other features of The Academy, a desirable educational experience mocks the students from the inaccessible periphery of ideality, or from behind the wall of a fiction novel that the teacher may be reading for leisure or hallucinogenic escape.

I witnessed another iteration of androidal vacancy in one of the math teachers, Mr. Johnson, a white man in his early fifties. He did not appear weak like the other teachers. Instead, he seemed as if he were on the verge of imploding. He harbored an unbridled, anxious irascibility, and expressed it often toward the students, who met him with equal ferocity. On a particular day Mr. Wheeler asked me to attend him to go to Mr. Johnson's classroom, which he remarked to me was known for always being in a "state of chaos." He and I traversed the main hallway, then turned left down one of two slim ducts. The journey felt imperiled by a sense of barrenness and foreboding. The walls were undecorated, the open space lightless, and the air stale. We turned what seemed to be an interminable number of abrupt corners, before we finally arrived to our destination. We emerged into the room to find Mr. Johnson on a bit of a warpath. His hair was disheveled, his face was red with frustration, and his eyes were unnaturally dilated. He was pacing back and forth in the room, on a tirade. The cadence of his steps was quick and nervous. He angrily told Agnes to move. She refused and yelled, "I hate you." She continued to repeat this antagonism several times. I took a seat at a table to observe. Mr. Johnson told me indignantly, "You have to move." I began to heed his directive. As I did so, Agnes and her friends demanded that I "sit right there." I moved anyway. The battle continued as Agnes and her gang casted aspersions upon the teacher. As he marched over to the telephone posted on the wall, he threatened to call security on them. Within a span of three minutes, he had gone over to the telephone and made two calls. Mr. Wheeler and I eventually left.

At that point in my visit, and even as I compose these words, I encounter another intuitional dilemma. I left the room with an overall impression that was not easily fitted to discourses of reason. In my fieldnotes I recorded the impression as a "bad vibe." Mr. Johnson left me feeling as if I had encountered hatred and evil in their most unadulterated forms. I had pangs of nervousness undulating in my chest as I walked back down the hallway. His body language, the quality of his eyes, and the undefinable ether that was being emitted from his pores suggested to me that he had a profound hatred for these students. Pregnant with the incessant murmur of anxiety in my chest, I was compelled to express how I felt to Mr. Wheeler:

Me: "There was not a good energy in that math class."

Mr. Wheeler: "The student going to The Grant School [pseudonym for a relatively reputable high school in the city] entered the sixth grade with a four [a four is the highest score attainable on a given state examination] and now has a one [the lowest score attainable]. The boy complained about the teacher, but nothing happened. They [the students] have him for three consecutive periods a day, so a lot of students are in danger of failing the exam."

Me: "Why do the students have him for so many periods throughout the day?"

Mr. Wheeler: "This is a Title I school, meaning that the state determines the curriculum. Failing schools have to have ten periods of math and ten periods of ELA per week. This means that each student only gets four periods of science in a week. This takes away from science time. But no one [those in charge of the curriculum] cares about science. No one cares if they [students] fail it."

At this point, a little context is necessary. Middle school students in New York have the option of applying to the high schools of their choice. This process is very much like that of applying for college admissions. Students are evaluated on grades, tests scores, the admissions essays they write, behavior records, and other supplementary material (e.g., art portfolios). If a student has gained admission to a particular school, that school can revoke its decision if the student achieves substandard grades or test scores in his or her final year of middle school. Thus, the relation stated earlier between a teacher's administered curriculum and a student's life prospects is an actual correlation—one of which at least two students in this study were aware.

In observing Mr. Johnson's behavior over the course of several months, and especially on the day just related, it was obvious how any student would have been repulsed by his demeanor, and therefore unreceptive to the subject matter. Yet Mr. Wheeler's comments raise other concerns.

The state had determined that The Academy had to have ten periods of math and ten periods of ELA weekly. Although I was not afforded the opportunity to speak with students and teachers directly regarding their respective attitudes about this course volume, I evoke a crude common sense to make a few conjectures. It would be reasonable to imagine that the student who has a natural aversion to math, for instance, would be mentally and emotionally exhausted from having to attend math classes ten times a week. It would also be reasonable to imagine that even the student who is moderately to exceedingly interested in math would have an aversion to taking that ominous journey down that narrow duct twenty times per week (ten to travel there and ten to leave) to attend the same class. The torment becomes even more pronounced if one is living with the realization that this class presents a hindrance to his or her intellectual and social possibilities.

The entire situation would become a burden for the teacher as well. That teacher has to make that same ominous journey every day. In every exchange with the students, the teacher would have to confront their subtextual understandings of the environment they must routinely inhabit, and the imposition of assumptions about who they are. This subtext would manifest as a general ennui, unruliness, violence—veritable chaos. The teacher must look forward to this predicament ten times per week. Both the students and the teacher would be locked inside of an infernal feedback loop. It is reasonable to imagine then that any aversions (such as a natural disdain for math or English), feelings of inadequacy (e.g., insecurity about mathematical or reading ability), and character imperfections (e.g., perhaps a teacher has a bad temper) would be magnified in such a feedback loop, which completes ten cycles per week as opposed to the four of a subject that is deemed marginal. The perpetuity of this feedback loop, made infinitely more infernal by its sub-tending symbolic structures of racist oppression and masochistic fantasy, offers a robust portrait of the Title I school, and of what Tyson Lewis refers to as "the deadening nature of national standardized testing movements" (2010).

These rituals prove to be deadening for both students and teachers. In fact, many of the teachers at The Academy throughout my period of observation exhibited dissociative, androidal behavior. They were dissociated from the material that they were teaching, their students, and even themselves. The students wanted the experience of humanization; yet their longings were, at every turn, thwarted. What they actually encountered were dissociative beings, androids and immense voids. If they desired academic and social advancement and teachers to provide them with these opportunities, yet these teachers were thwarting these possibilities and reneging on these promises, then students routinely encountered enemies, guilty of the most unpardonable forms of treason. "Unwanted," "bad," "unintelligent," "hated," "betrayed," "uncared for," "unlikely to succeed" were the tropological densities that became affixed to the denizens of the ironic fourth dimension of The Academy, confirming Signithia Fordham's thesis that schooling "implant[s] the values and cultural norms of the dominant Other" (1996). To these densities were added the ones deemed most important for district officials and the constituted "F-ness" of The Academy: the state examination scores.

Chapter Six

The ELA State Examination

The day of the New York State English Language Arts (ELA) examination at The Academy appeared to be rather anticlimactic. That day had not the air of importance, of ceremony, that one would have expected. It did not feel like a region of experience that had been ritually delimited in space and time. There were hardly any sacred objects, no high priestesses, and no profound mysteries into which a young neophyte could be absorbed. There was only the muck and desolation of a typical day.

There were some alterations made to the total atmosphere, however. Students were herded into various classrooms, different from the ones they were accustomed to attending in the first period of every morning. Apart from the room changes, not much was different. In one particular classroom, which was the terminal chamber of one of the narrow ducts, there sat about forty students. Crystal entered. She was gesticulating passionately as she related a story to Mr. Wheeler. Although I could not make out the content of the exchange, I gleaned from the harshness of her voice and the general aggressiveness of her movements that she was angry. The weight of her hostility filled the whole room. Rather than attempting to calm her down, Mr. Wheeler simply stated, half to Crystal and half to me, "One day I'm going to come to my class and find a parent laid out in front of my door." I asked him to clarify. He told me that "one day a parent is going to come and beat the shit out of one of these teachers!" I gathered that Crystal's diatribe related to a conflict that she had had with one of the faculty members. Mr. Wheeler apparently found the girl's reaction to be warranted.

In a separate region of the room, another girl was being disruptive. One "weak" teacher, Mrs. Warren, encouraged her to "take her seat," but the girl refused. With a hostile, determined apostrophe, such as is the chosen manner of expression at times for teenagers in New York City, the girl proclaimed, "I

am not taking the test because I don't like the proctor." Mr. Wheeler analyzed this comment for me: "These kids are so personal that they withdraw if
they don't like a teacher. They think they are hurting you by not taking their
test. They don't understand that they are only hurting themselves."

There was the usual din of disruption in the room. Yet, present was also a
general abandonment of reverence for the day and the test itself. Mr. Wheeler
at an opportune moment pulled two boys aside and told them with encouragement and firm conviction, "This is a very important day. This is the state
test. This counts toward your passage to the eighth grade." The boys both
responded, "I got you," meaning, "I understand."

I accompanied Mr. Wheeler to another classroom, which appeared to be
even more disorderly than the first. The students were boisterously engaged
in conversation throughout, boys were play-fighting, and students were hurl-
ing projectiles across the room. The lead teacher—white, female, middle-
aged, with noticeably dark circles around her eyes—in the room made several lackluster attempts to bring order to the chaos. Written in her eyes was a
record of some most egregious assault on humanity. Bearing witness to such
a thing had left her—mouth agape, eyes perpetually dilated in disbelief and
angst—transfixed in a state of horror. Her chidings had no impact. She proceeded to read the instructions for the test as the booklets were being distributed. She held the papers as if they would somehow protect her from the
possibility of human intimacy, or perhaps the threat of an untoward remark.
The test officially began, yet there was no officialness. There was no boundary demarcated in time and circumstance that separated the general melee
from the structured environment of the test. The test and the chaos were all a
part of the same dilapidated structure. The atmosphere did eventually achieve
a prevailing sense of placidity, nevertheless. Occasionally there would be
outbursts of laughter, or other willful assertions of anger.

The open door permitted the noise in the hallway to enter and disturb the
already tenuous tranquility. One girl exclaimed, "I can't concentrate! Can
somebody close the door!?" Mrs. Warren stepped into the hallway and
shushed the offenders. They complied. The girl smacked her lips, but did not
offer a "Thank you." Three girls asked for Mrs. Warren's assistance, or
rather issued insolent commands at various points. They smacked their lips
and rolled their eyes as they did so. After Mrs. Warren attended to them, they
simply resumed their work with no offerings of gratitude. At one point a
student released flatulence, which caused the entire room to erupt in a mix-
ture of laughter and disgust. Many left their seats and scurried to the perimeter of the room. A teacher, Mrs. Leevy, an African American woman in her
mid-forties, walked into the room, and, glaring at the students, reprimanded
them in assertive, official discourse: "You can be held accountable for cheat-
ing if you are talking." There is no resistance to her chidings. She continued:
"This is not a game! This is the state exam!" She continued to glare at the

students until they had returned to a state of relative sobriety. Not content that equanimity had been fully restored, Mr. Wheeler continued to glare at the flatulent offender until the latter had assumed a disposition of complete seriousness. The silence of the room had now become absolute. Mrs. Leevy and Mr. Wheeler had lent to the moment the rigid, yet volatile contours of a sacred occasion.

The ELA state examination, one of two epifocal moments over the course of a nine-month process (the other being the state math examination), assumed a character incommensurate with the emphasis that the New York City Department of Education placed upon the test prior to and beyond the actual date of administration. For example, Mr. Wheeler said of Crystal's prospects for the ELA state examination, "She is a '4.' Now we are worried that she will get a '2' because of that lady [Mrs. Beal]." The grammatical structure of the statement, "She is a 4," is telling. Similar to what I had witnessed on several occasions in my general observations of schools and school-affiliated institutions around the city, in Crystal's case, symmetry was established between student and score.

How could it be, then, that an event critical to one's matriculation through the educational edifice, a predictor of one's social prospects, and a focal point of identity, be treated as a moment without urgency, consequence, or even utility? If even those students regarded as having a good chance of succeeding (e.g., Crystal) felt unprepared due to the inferior quality of the teaching, it is reasonable to suspect that the majority of the students also felt unprepared. And if the students' accusations that Mrs. Beal "does not teach" have any merit, and my observations of her generally dissociative impulses are accurate, then it is also reasonable to assume that perhaps throughout the period of time leading up to the exam, Mrs. Beal had not been able to effectively instill the value of the exam to her students. I would imagine then that students' feelings of unpreparedness and a general feeling that their teacher had no earnest interest in ensuring their preparedness conspired to divest the test and its administration of any seriousness or positive significance.

Or, perhaps the test did have a positive significance. The students probably recognized that, to those who were prepared, who had caring teachers, the test had all the significance of a tool of academic and social advancement. On test day, however, one of the most unconscionable acts of legerdemain imaginable was committed. Each exam was distributed. With each one was a ticket of admission to a reputable high school and a road out of poverty. As soon as the test was opened, however, the ticket instantly disappeared. What was left before these students was a montage of images, judgments, understandings, and forecastings. There were teachers who do not "care," a "bad school," a sub-human experience, limited prospects, an "F," a "1." Indeed, the test booklet was not a sacrament of any sort; nor was it a mundane, utilitarian tool. It was not even a pointless particle of debris. It was the antithesis of all that is sacrosanct, the densest point of convergence for all that is unutterably dangerous and profane. And these objects were ubiquitous, occupying a central position on everyone's desk. The students withdrew—physically, cognitively, and emotionally—from this object, before and during the time that it lay haughtily across their desks. The students handled the booklet, confronted the horror for one hour and then they were done.

Up to this point we have mentioned a few defining moments in which bad faith would achieve a type of inertia in its cyclical continuum between itself and good faith, a restive moment of ontological closure. There was the primary closure of the racist symbolic order, the tropological achievement of the bad school through statistical measurements, and to an extent, Mrs. Beal's leisure reading during class time. To these, we must add another, the day of the ELA state examination itself. For on this day, students' lack of preparation would manifest itself as substandard test scores, which would then be fed into a sophisticated formula to determine the fate of each one and the status of the school itself. Test day completes the cycle, for it is the very occasion that ossifies the construct of "the bad school," which in turn establishes the ontological closure of "bad students," "bad teachers," and the like. In Durkheimian fashion, the ritual of the state test lends an inalienable solidity to the symbolic configurations that were inevitably a part of that ritual.[1] The actual taking of the test constitutes a Turnerian liminal period (1969, 1974, 1985, 1992), a cauldron in which symbolic configurations can be altered or emerge anew. But alas, liminality did not beget novel innovation, but rather a more profound intransigence to existing symbolic forms.

Based upon the analysis in previous chapters, we might interpret the students' unorthodox behavior during the test as an expression of utopic discontent. The foregoing evidence would suggest that this judgment is valid. However, we must not forget the entire field of beings available to the students at The Academy, and, by extension, on test day. The students could assume the mantle of badness, iconoclasm (see chapter 6 for an explanation of the unfeasibility of this choice), and the dialectical resolution of the two, utopic discontent. "Good student" would reside, as established in chapter 3, in the fourth dimension of ideality, offering a defining counterpoint to the bad school.

The students' choice of badness during the administration of the ELA State Exam was practically inevitable. Sabrina Zirkel contends that, in the wake of *Brown v. Board of Education*, black students in particular continue to retain the "stigma" of inferiority. As a result, students align themselves with this stigma as if it were a prescription or some type of inevitability (2005). Dave Moscinski defines this as No Child Left Behind's "Pygmalion Effect"—teachers formulate low expectations of their students' academic abilities, and in response, students internalize and become the image that is projected (2008). Regarding the ontological closure of the test-day anti-ritual itself, there is evidence that such events can intensify a student's awareness of these negative projections, having the result of compromising academic performance (Blascovich, Spencer, Quinn, and Steele 2001; Contrada et al. 2000, 2001; Gougis 1986).

Within the field of total potential being in The Academy, test day constituted a regionally defined subset of beings and choices. Excepting the small minority of students who might have been able to map some idiosyncratic route to a good performance (although we must be reminded of the fact that, as per my conversations with Mr. Wheeler, students who entered the school year with high marks declined considerably), the majority of the students could only choose to fail. Either they chose not to make an earnest attempt to succeed, thereby ensuring failure, or they chose to take the test in earnest, even though failure was next to inevitable.

Yet, within this grand vehicle of inevitability, in which the ontological closure of badness was virtually guaranteed, there was one grand foil to it all—an iconoclast, resisting this closure, and exhibiting a religious fervor counter to that of the parishioners in the religion of the bad school: Mr. Wheeler.

NOTE

1. Refer to Durkheim's discussions of totemic rituals and collective effervescence in *Elementary Forms of Religious Life* (2001).

Chapter Seven

Mr. Wheeler

If many of the other teachers in The Academy were androids, Mr. Wheeler was an excessive humanity. His eyes were never vacant, nervous, inert, or acquiescent. They were, at all times, full of light and vigor, meaningfully engaged with every aspect of their immediate environment. His walk and his general disposition carried a sense of purpose and sturdiness. His words were never inaudible, but resounded with a boom and sass that could pierce, dissolve, or create whatever took residence behind their intention. Yet the seam binding the resonant boom, the perpetual urgency and sturdiness, was a quiet indestructibility. There was nothing volatile and unsteadied in his urgency. The subtext of his existence was that any confrontation with him, large or small, would inevitably result in the demise of the antagonist, never Mr. Wheeler. His carriage was of one who was apodictically certain about his power, indomitability, talent, and genius. This certainty granted him a license to be transparent and human in ways that could very well have guaranteed the demise of one with less assuredness.

He was "from the streets" and the students were all aware of this fact. If he did not like another teacher, he had no problem letting this fact be known publicly. If a student "stepped" to him disrespectfully, he was subject to return the hostility through strategically placed wit, for which he had a particular penchant. He had an insider's knowledge of "how things work" in urban ghettos. He had grown up in one in New York City, successfully navigated his way out of it, and had devoted his life to changing the educational outcomes of children from disadvantaged communities throughout New York City and beyond. He spoke to the students, frankly and in graphic (never inappropriate) detail, about his own experiences and those he had witnessed or about which he had heard. He initiated and welcomed a range of conversation topics from his students, from the mundane to the frighteningly egregious. His reactions were always visceral and honest, never concealed beneath a veil of pretense or professional reticence. If he did not like something, he would say so, without euphemism or apology.

He was cut from the same cloth as many of them were, yet was, by far, not their peer. He treated no subject as if it were a trivial matter for idle discourse. His insight was very much that of a domestically and globally informed citizen—a perspective that was quite exhilarating for the students. Mr. Wheeler could always connect the here-and-now with the goings-on of the nation and the world. He had a natural aptitude for such global analysis, to which the students willingly and quite naturally deferred.

He was also openly and unapologetically feminine. In fact, he lived quite organically within his effeminacy. Neither students nor teachers dared insult him as a result of his choice of comportment.

Like many educators, Mr. Wheeler carried the assumption that students' needs take precedence in an educational setting. However, he carried equally that the teacher deserves the same degree of consideration and personal respect. He gave all to his students, but never at the expense of his own dignity and self-worth. For Mr. Wheeler, placing one's self in the service of another does not mean that one is required to be the victim of diminution.

What emerged most powerfully from the ethnographic record about Mr. Wheeler, however, was not the texture of his voice, his manner of communicating, or any aspect of his outward comportment. What shone through most poignantly was the fact that he was a paragon of virtue. As I said earlier, he was transparent, with nothing to hide. Not only his toughness, but the rectitude of his system of values, gave him permission to be transparent. As will be presently illustrated, the values to which Mr. Wheeler subscribed and his philosophy of education lent him a degree of positive influence in the lives of the students that was unattainable for many of the other teachers.

One of the most prominent aspects of the data that I collected was the preponderance of instances in which Mr. Wheeler would transform moments of academic difficulty or discord into opportunities to instill various aspects of his value system. For instance, on an occasion in which he was explaining a particular exercise in scientific method and data collection that the students were in the process of completing, a girl lamented that she had "made a mistake." Mr. Wheeler, with a graceful, yet purposeful and expectant ease, pointed toward the back wall of the classroom, where hung a brightly colored aphorism. He asked the girl to read it aloud. She proceeded: "He who has never made a mistake, has never tried anything new." Mr. Wheeler continued by telling the class that "mistakes are good": "Mistakes are the foundation of science. If we scientists did not make mistakes, then we wouldn't learn anything new." His words cast a silence over the room, after which time he proceeded to complete his explanation of the assignment. Not only did his exegesis of "mistakes" prove significant for the assignment at hand, but his chidings carried the weight of a lesson that could be incorporated into one's character, informing his or her general approach to difficulties. The lesson was simultaneously about the virtue of perseverance and the detriment of self-debasement. He delivered his ministrations with a solidity and authority that bespoke of an intention to make the words have a permanent impact.

If the students' scholastic existence was overcast with the dull hues of non-ideality, Mr. Wheeler was perpetually engaged in making that existence one of vibrant possibilities. Every lifeless hue Mr. Wheeler existentially displaced with one that was more pleasing to human sensibilities. Illustrative of this existential displacement was Mr. Wheeler's relationship to a student named Gerald. On a particular day, Gerald, a well-mannered, amicable, tall young man of African American descent, walked past Mr. Wheeler and me. Mr. Wheeler entreated Gerald to come back so that he and I could meet. Mr. Wheeler introduced us, at which point the boy extended his hand to shake mine. He told Gerald that I was going to help him with his letter. I was a bit caught off guard, but followed along anyway (it was Mr. Wheeler's way to keep people alert using unexpected gestures, randomly distributed). He looked at Gerald expectantly, "Are you going to tell Mr. Parker what the letter is about?" The boy told me that the letter was an appeal to the school to overlook his age—he was sixteen at the time—so that he could play on the basketball team. I noticed that the boy spoke with a stutter. He shook my hand, then left. Mr. Wheeler then addressed me, "Did you notice that he stutters?" I answered, "Yes." He continued:

"Gerald is one of the smartest kids in the school, but he thinks it is not cool to be intelligent. Because he is one of the cool kids, he doesn't want to work. It is not cool to be black and smart. I make him speak to other people as often as he can so that he can feel comfortable doing so. I want him to be able to speak to administrators. He needs to have the attitude, 'I don't care if I stutter. You are going to listen to me. You are just going to have to wait and listen to what I have to say.'"

What constituted a mark of shame for Gerald and threatened to preclude his ability to advocate for himself, Mr. Wheeler converted into a protest for the acknowledgment of deserved humanity. In addition, Mr. Wheeler was actively enlarging the boy's possibilities within and beyond The Academy by helping him to confront what could potentially remain a lifelong hindrance. Mr. Wheeler was very self-consciously giving Gerald the tools to transcend the conditions of oppression.

Consistent with observations in previous chapters, Gerald's disengagement from a scholarly identity is indeed an extension of the embedded racist tropology of The Academy.[1] Gerald's decision to hide his intelligence and underperform in school in order to be "cool" are symptomatic of particular negative tropes concerning black men who are a part of the governing symbolic order. Gillman Whiting attributes black male underperformance in academic institutions to the failure of the larger society, schools, and individual teachers to effectively wed a "scholarly identity" specifically to the notion of a black male identity (2006). Essential to this positive formulation of black male identity is what Bandura calls "self-efficacy," which is the belief that "I can do it; I am competent and able" (1977). A cultural trend persists in which black males are encouraged to have a tremendous amount of self-efficacy concerning sports, music and entertainment, yet not with respect to academic pursuits (Whiting 2006).

Mr. Wheeler was able to actively nurture Gerald's sense of self-efficacy because he understood and empathized with the larger social implications of Gerald's chosen identity within The Academy. Mr. Wheeler practiced what Ladson-Billings referred to as "culturally relevant pedagogy," in which the teacher uses his or her understanding of students' cultures as a basis for instruction (1995). Furthermore, Gerald's and Mr. Wheeler's exchanges were first and foremost founded upon a healthy student-faculty relationship that transcended classroom learning proper. Mr. Wheeler took a personal interest in Gerald's well-being. Mr. Wheeler's practices are consistent with research that establishes a causal link between teachers' healthy relationships with their students and the formers' increased capacity to encourage positive academic practices (Gloria and Robinson-Kurpius, 2001) and discourage maladaptive behavior outside the classroom (Adams and Singh 1998; Lonczak et al. 2001, 2002; McNeely et al. 2002; Sanders and Jordan 2000).

Mr. Wheeler's ability to positively influence the total well-being of his students and to transform the immediate environment into one full of propitious existential possibilities would often assume a tone of humor and vernacular wit. On one occasion a girl expressed an opinion (the content of which I cannot now recall) that elicited disagreeable outbursts from the students. Mr. Wheeler commanded their silence with the piercing boom of his voice. He then asked, "Who agrees with her?" His questions prompted an uneven distribution of raised hands. He then asked one of the objectors why he disagreed. After the boy's explanation, Mr. Wheeler asked others whether or not they agreed. Open, unstructured disagreement erupted throughout the room. Mr. Wheeler intervened a second time: "Uh uh! Don't be ghetto and say, 'I wanna fight her because she disagreed with me!'" Laughter ensued. He then modeled how to express differences of opinion, "When you disagree with people in the world, you have to say, 'Excuse me, but I disagree.'" He then demanded that everyone in the class express objections in this very way for the duration of that discussion. For the most part, they all complied. Mr. Wheeler, in all the time that I spent in The Academy, never once *asked* for the students' willing compliance to the values that he regarded highly. He always demanded it. Rarely did a student attempt to transgress these orders in his presence.

These existential transformations would, at times, assume a particularly political character. There were several instances in the ethnographic record, for instance, in which Mr. Wheeler gave social and historical significance to seemingly insignificant comments or behaviors. During one class period Mr. Wheeler and Mrs. Beal were collaborating on a particular lesson. The former emerged into the latter's classroom to find that students were exhibiting their routine disruptive behavior. Mr. Wheeler immediately began a string of reprimands: "I demand good conduct. I demand excellence." He forced students to make eye contact with his own expectant, reproachful gaze: "I also demand respect!" He found a small enclave of girls in the back of the classroom, pointed to a more central position in the room, and commanded them, "Move here! I don't take that garbage." As they found their way to the center of the room, he addressed Mrs. Beal about another group of students sitting in the back of the classroom, "Did you put them there?" She shook her head, at which point he positioned himself at the front of the room and began speaking in a loud, assertive manner:

"Black and Latino youth who sit at the back of the classroom are 75 percent more in danger of failing. And Rosa Parks sat at the front of the bus so we can sit in the front in school and everywhere else. Stop sitting in the back!"

At that point, he told them, "Get to work!" They all became silent and began working dutifully. When Mr. Wheeler exited permanently, however, the students resumed their untoward behavior. Mrs. Beal attempted half-heartedly and ineffectually to bring them to task.

The simple ritual of students congregating in the back of the classroom had been infused with tropological import. The geography of the room became a racial, socio-historical tableau of various existential possibilities. If a student were to sit in the back of the room, that one was choosing historical retrogression and present social demise. Sitting in a central or front position, conversely, became a gesture of historical progress and a guarantee of present social ascendency. The silence with which the students received Mr. Wheeler's admonition and their willingness to comply with his directive to relocate probably indicates that they had also complied with his reconstitution of the room's geography along existential, racial, social, and historical axes.

Mr. Wheeler's speech is reminiscent of bell hooks's meditation upon her own experiences when she attended a segregated school. hooks described the black teachers as having a "messianic zeal to transform our minds and beings." In her departure to white schools, she found that the teachers would confirm racist stereotypes and the pedagogical experience itself would become sterile, "about information only" (1994). Mr. Wheeler acted in the tradition of those pre-segregation teachers that hooks and Kelly (2010) discuss. In addition, in moments such as the one just related, Mr. Wheeler would seek to instill a distinctly positive sense of ethnic identity, a practice that educational scholars have consistently confirmed as advantageous to students' self-esteem and academic performance (Carlson, Uppal, and Prosser 2000; Helms 1990; Phinney, Cantu, and Kurz 1997; Phinney and Chavira 1992; Phinney, Chavira, and Williamson 1992; Rowley et al. 1998; Sellers, Rowley, Chavous, Shelton, and Smith 1997).

Mr. Wheeler was not only adept at reconstituting the tropo-geography of the classroom, but also that of the broader social matrix of the state of New York. During one of his classes, for instance, he overheard a girl talking to a group of friends, saying: "I was going to move to Long Island, where all the white schools are." Lydia then said, "If I went to a white school, my grades would be 'dumb good'[2] and my behavior would be 'dumb good.'" Looking in their direction, Mr. Wheeler made an address, half to the girls and half to the entire class: "Why do you down yourselves? By saying that, you let people know that you think black and Latino schools are inferior to white schools." He then asked rhetorically, "What makes a difference between you doing your work and behaving well here and doing the same at a white school?" All were silent. He put the question to the girls who made the statements. He framed the questions more insistently, repeating them to the girls and to other select individuals in the class. None of them had any responses. Mr. Wheeler saw rather astutely that the girls had assigned negative value to the densities "black," "Latino," and by extension, "me" and everything intimately associated with these configurations (e.g., The Academy). By contrast, they had assigned positive value to "white" and all entities with which that density was intimately associated (e.g., Long Island). By clearly identifying and articulating this subtext of the girls' conversation, Mr. Wheeler was able to disaggregate the former set of densities from negativity and infuse them with a positive valuation. He was adhering to what hooks might call a "messianic zeal."

In addition to his more explicit procedures of reconstitution, Mr. Wheeler performed tacit ones as well, particularly in the quotidian rituals of the classroom. On a certain day in which students were working collaboratively on an assignment, he related to me that "this method of teaching [group work] is unconventional for me." He then explained that he allowed them to work in groups because he knew that they would be tempted to speak socially to one another. "I want to teach them that even though you are having fun or you have a crisis, the world continues to move forward and the work is still due. If they catch on, they learn how to prioritize for themselves, because the bottom line is that the work is still due. You learn to work first and talk later, or talk while you work." Through the tool of group work, Mr. Wheeler would manufacture a situation in which students were forced not only to choose their fate, but assume complete responsibility for the consequences of their choices.

Teaching students to excel in the midst of distractions and difficulties was at the core of Mr. Wheeler's philosophy of education. In a particular conversation that I had with him, I asked him about his decision to teach science. He said to me that the primary reason that he wanted to teach the subject was that it is generally regarded as difficult. He continued, "All a child needs is to succeed at one thing they thought they would not succeed at. To pass a science test is just that. That's what life is. . . . In meeting difficult situations and succeeding in them, I am teaching them how to struggle. I am teaching them how to be self-accountable."

Teaching the students how to "struggle" was, from my observations, an integral part of the time that students spent in Mr. Wheeler's class. On one particular day, I witnessed several exchanges that exemplified this theme. At the very beginning of the class, students walked in to take their seats. They proceeded to speak to one another socially. Mr. Wheeler positioned himself behind his desk and asked sarcastically, "Why are people not working?" He proceeded, "Your assignment is due at the end of class. Let's go!" The students immediately rearranged themselves at the tables, pulled out their books and worksheets, and began to work. As they began, Mr. Wheeler exclaimed, "Your coats!" Many of them immediately left their seats and hung their coats on hooks that had been newly affixed to the book shelves. Mr. Wheeler explained to me that he required students to hang up their coats now as a symbolic gesture of immersing themselves completely into the experience of learning. Pointedly to one girl who had remained seated, he implored her, "Stay a while." She immediately left her seat to hang up her coat.

A few more minutes into the class, Mr. Wheeler stepped into a special storage area, gathered several white laptop computers and deposited them on a table positioned at the front of the room. One girl asked him about a particular question on her worksheet. He told her to look up the answer on one of the computers. She went to the laptop. He then said to me, "I am trying to provide access. I know that if they learn how to research for themselves, they will be set for the rest of their lives."

Toward the end of class, a boy asked Mr. Wheeler for a pencil. Annoyed, he said, "I'm not giving you a pencil in the last ten minutes of class. What were you doing for the first part of the class?" Another student at his table answered for the boy, "Talking." In fact, all the boys had been talking for the whole class. Mr. Wheeler had made it very clear to the students in his class that he did not reward habits and behaviors that do not adhere to his high standards. The boy was unable to contest Mr. Wheeler's verdict.

A little later, a girl returned to Mr. Wheeler, expressing bafflement at several questions. He entreated her to sit at his desk. He began by asking her a litany of questions. In the silences and in response to her complaints of being confused, Mr. Wheeler instructed her to "try to figure it out." Perpetually, he placed the onus of solving problems onto the students.

In the final moments of the class, a student approached Mr. Wheeler and asked in a tone of uncertainty: "Can you give me the sheet that you gave. . . . " Mr. Wheeler interrupted him, "What sheet? Look at your rubric and tell me what you need." The boy returned to his desk. Mr. Wheeler said to me emphatically, "Communication." The boy returned with a slip of paper, which he showed to Mr. Wheeler. The boy pointed to an item and said, "That one." Mr. Wheeler said, "I don't know what 'that one' is. Tell me what you need." The boy then read something off the sheet. Mr. Wheeler told him that he had already completed this assignment. The boy then contested, "I need 'Rocks and Minerals.'" Mr. Wheeler then handed him a cluster of worksheets.

By teaching students the values of communicative facility, self-accountability, struggling and remaining focused in the midst of distractions, Mr. Wheeler was imparting lessons that he knew would help them transcend the domain of non-ideality. At other times he understood that he had to achieve this transcendence on their behalf. On two occasions in particular, Mr. Wheeler evoked a strategic passivity as a means of directly altering the students' material circumstances. On a day in which a school assembly was occurring, for instance, a white male teacher, Mr. Barry, was trying to coax a recalcitrant Andy into attending. The latter refused to go unless Mr. Wheeler consented to accompany him. Andy then asked Mr. Wheeler if he was attending, to which the latter replied, "Yes." Mr. Wheeler smiled. Mr. Barry then whispered to Mr. Wheeler, "I know you don't like to put them in check, but sometimes you have to." This accusation began somewhat of an intense exchange:

Mr. Wheeler: "Do you know why I don't?"

Mr. Barry: "No."

Mr. Wheeler: "Because he will end up in the hall. Do you know what will happen?"

Mr. Barry: "What?"

Mr. Wheeler: "They will suspend him. I don't want to hand him over to people who don't care about him."

Mr. Wheeler then turned away from Mr. Barry and asked Andy, "What's the problem?" He simply stated that he did not want to go with Mr. Barry. Mr. Wheeler told the boy to go with Mr. Barry and he would meet him in the auditorium. Mr. Wheeler said, "Go where we usually sit."

In another scenario, Mrs. Beal entered Mr. Wheeler's classroom on several occasions in the span of twenty minutes, asking him to attend a meeting in the principal's office. He told her that he was in the middle of a lesson and that he would come when he was done. With each time that she entered, he became sharper and firmer, until the situation boiled to a climax. Interpreting her repeated emergence as rude interruptions, he addressed her with a tone of overt disdain, "I am in the middle of a lesson and will come when I am finished." Upon her exit, the students let out a unanimous, "Ooooh." After he had finished his explanation, he indicated to me that he was not going to attend the meeting: "That conference is about kicking two students out, two black boys. I will not be used to kick black students out. That's why they [the adults in the school] don't like me . . . because I am defiant."

Excessive suspensions and expulsions were common practice at The Academy, a microcosm of a larger phenomenon in urban school districts. For example, the rate at which minority students are expelled (Toppo 2011) and suspended (Abdul-Aleem 2011) far exceeds that for white students. Racial discrimination has been cited as a powerful motivator for these practices. In addition, excising students from school on a temporary or a permanent basis has been shown to be a causative prelude to their encounter with the juvenile and criminal justice systems (Abdul-Aleem 2011).

Paradoxically, when a minority student is excommunicated from a "bad school," she or he simultaneously becomes nuclear to the symbolic order itself. That student becomes the densest point of articulation along a trajectory that had already ensured that point's deracination from humanity, its progressive objectification, and disposability. It follows then that the negation of a student's humanity would result in a more abundant form of negation: expulsion or suspension. The punitive excision of the student from a pedagogical setting, therefore, is but another moment of ontological closure, in which not only the symbolic order, but also the trope of the "bad school," achieves relative inertia.

Mr. Wheeler's disarming of The Academy's inertia manifested itself in the manner in which he would invest in his students emotionally. On one occasion he confessed to me, "I do get stressed when I get a kid like Andy because I have this funny feeling that he is going to get killed. And no matter what I say, he just doesn't get it. I do lose sleep over that boy."

At times I was struck by how well he could detect that his students were held under the weight of some affliction. He sensed, for instance, during the beginning of one class that two girls were deeply perturbed. Having observed these girls on several occasions, I had not noticed a significant change in their demeanor. Mr. Wheeler, however, could see clearly that something was wrong. He immediately called them into the hallway. He asked them what was troubling them. Neither of them was forthcoming. He continued to prod them, "It's all over your face. I can tell when something is wrong." One girl finally broke her silence. She paused, and then called Mr. Wheeler away from the door. He then closed the door so that other people could not hear. One of the girls proceeded to tell him about a conflict between students at The Academy and those at a neighboring school. The girl had friends on both sides of the dispute. After listening for about three minutes, he asked, "What do you want me to do about it?" There was no answer. He then filled in the silence, "I'll talk to them. I'll take care of it." He then handed them their assignment, gave them instructions, and told them to go inside.

That moment may be regarded as a microcosm of all the relationships that Mr. Wheeler had nurtured with his students, and coincidentally, as the accomplishment of a seemingly impossible feat of human engagement: he assumed complete accountability for his students, yet paradoxically, challenged them to be completely self-accountable. For he acknowledged that the girls' burden was a formidable one, so, out of concern, he offered to relieve it himself. Yet in handing them their assignment, he tacitly reinforced another lesson: "The work is still due."

NOTES

1. For an example of an anthropological study of NCLB's effects on gender and racial identity, refer to Chikkatur (2012).

2. In New York City teenager slang, "dumb" used in this way approximately indicates "extremely" or "very."

Chapter Eight

Being Toward Eradication

School Closing and Gentrification

In 2008, two years after the completion of my fieldwork, The Academy closed for good, with a tragic sense of inevitability and without circumstance, much like the conclusion of the English Language Arts (ELA) State Examinations. Nothing much else could have been expected from a bad school; it had no weaponry to challenge the school's most formidable opponent, a racist symbolic order. The space where The Academy used to be was immediately supplanted by a well-performing school that had already been in residence in that building; the latter simply expanded its franchise to that lightless domain so that it had even more space to increase its level of productivity. In his three terms in office, Mayor Michael Bloomberg had closed 140 schools in New York City, with seventeen more slated to close in 2013 (Johnson 2013). Despite these facts, the phenomena of school closing and phase-out in New York City remains grossly understudied. Notwithstanding this lack of scholarly attention, residents in New York, particularly those who have experienced the closing of their children's schools, concur that the loss of a school in one's community has profound personal, social, and cultural consequences. Although the timing of my entry into the field did not allow me to bear witness to events surrounding the initial decision to close The Academy, I was able to conduct fieldwork in a nearby neighborhood that was fighting with the New York City Department of Education (DOE) regarding a decision to phase out one of its long-standing elementary schools.

The city called a number of meetings in which DOE representatives, called "advocates," met with auditoriums full of community members—parents, educators, activists, program administrators, and general well-wishers—to discuss the impending decision to close the school. Because these convocations were open to the general public, I was able to attend all of them as an inconspicuous spectator. By far the most vocal of all the attendants, the parents, a considerable number of whom had lived in the community for many years and sent multiple generations of children to that same school, made rather incisive observations about the relation between the imminent phase-out, its ramifications for the overall ethos of the community, its impact upon their children's well-being and future prospects, and the very existence of the community itself. In other words, the discourse surrounding the closing of that particular elementary school was inherently existential. The concerns arising most prominently in these meetings can be summarized as follows: (1) the closing of the school would upset very delicate social networks that had been nurtured over a period of decades; (2) the children would regress academically and would begin to exhibit disciplinary problems; (3) the children would experience a profound sense of loss once their school, trusted teachers, and administrators were no longer in place; (4) the parents' right to choose and to exercise their civil liberties would be compromised as a result of not having input in school board decisions; and (5) the closing of the school was part of larger gentrification efforts that would eventually ensure that the community itself would cease to exist.

If the doomed, transitory life of a bad school runs its course within the centripetal vector of our prevailing symbolic order, then the inevitable outcome of that process, the closing of a school, simultaneously allows that order to achieve an added degree of tropological inertia and to reverberate centrifugally. For the death of a school at once fulfills the tropological progression from non-human, to expendable object, terminating in non-entity, and hurtles the surrounding community along the same trajectory. What follows is a brief ethnographic account of one community's efforts to counter these progressions.

As the substance of this ethnographic encounter resides primarily in dialogic exchanges, in order to provide a sense of the voices and governing sentiments occasioning the closing of Community Elementary, I have chosen to reproduce at length the dialogue of the two most energized and representative of the public forums. The first two sections are primarily descriptive, while the subsequent two sections provide an analysis of the first two. The final section offers some concluding remarks.

FIRST SCHOOL CLOSING MEETING

The first of these convocations occurred in the school auditorium, which was situated on the ground floor. The venue served a dual purpose: its size was conducive to holding large numbers of people, and its relative grandeur lent the occasion a character of ritual formality. As is the architectural convention of auditoriums, the back of the structure, which was also the main point of entry, continued to the front in a downward slope, terminating at the stage. Along the way were several rows of seats, approximately 200 in all. By 6:30 p.m., the official start time, the auditorium was already nearly full. One could hear conversation that ranged from the carefree banter of familiars to all manners of aggrieved chatter among strangers who had formed ad hoc bonds of social and political camaraderie. The meeting had the air of a public forum, a democratic gathering. The facilitators, five of them, entered casually and positioned themselves between the front row of seats and the stage. Each of them was suited in the non-descript drapery of middle-management officialdom—gray, pleated skirts, black blazers, white or gray button-down shirts. They each brought with them a folder and shared two microphones among them. Their arrival shifted the democratic balance that had been the prevailing mode of relations in the room. There were now clear authorities and subordinates. Yet the authority was rather self-effacing and modest, as it chose to position itself below the stage, on the same terrain as the locals. At best, it was a tenuous, disingenuous sense of equivalency.

A little after 6:30, the facilitators began their predictable prefatory remarks: there was an official greeting, the announcement of the purpose of the meeting, and an introduction of each of the facilitators. They stated that the meeting was intended to answer the community's questions about the impending decision to close the school. One woman took the floor and asked in a mildly annoyed tone: "Why are you deciding to close the school now?" One facilitator answered in a manner that was almost patronizing in its professional sterility, "When a school is failing, it either changes leadership, phases out, or a combination of both. For Community Elementary School, we had already changed leadership. The Department of Education has now voted to phase the school out."

Another parent, offended by the response, emerged to her feet. "Why are you deciding to phase the school out now, when the outcome for this year, after the change in leadership, has yet to be seen?" She proceeded to say that the phase-out was a "function of the economic status in the community." With condescending didacticism, another facilitator rebutted, "Phase-outs occur all over New York City. They occur because schools are failing and not because of the economic status of the community." The woman would not be diminished, however. She reemerged to her feet, "Sir, I have a master's in public education and it is a known fact that phase-outs occur disproportionately in poor communities." To her repartee the facilitator had no response. She continued to insinuate that the school that was to be phased in was a charter school that would not serve the needs of the community.

A father stood and continued with this topic, "How do we know that the school that will be phased in will actually benefit this community?" To this question and others that were rather unanswerable, the droning refrain was some version of, "This is why we are holding this meeting. We want your voices to be heard so that the new school can accommodate your needs."

A young woman stood to her feet, indignant, "I want to know why you are deciding to phase the school out now, when the school has been failing for twelve years? What can we do to stop this from happening? You all are going to do what you want to do anyway. Protests are not going to get it reversed." A facilitator responded, "Let me clarify our role a bit. We are advocates for you. You can decide what type of school comes into this building, but you have to let your voices be heard in volume. The more voices that are heard, the more you are able to decide the fate of this building." The commiserative gestures did nothing to assuage the attendants' critical posture or transform their analyses (the facilitators might have used the word "perception"). As far as the former were concerned, these "advocates" were the vicars of the DOE.

Another community member took the floor: "They take away dance, athletics, afterschool tutoring, and a whole lot of other programs, and expect the kids to thrive. That doesn't make sense!"

Next, a father took the center aisle:

"I have seen a tremendous change in my son over the past month. His grades are going up and he is not misbehaving in class. He tells me all the time that he likes his principal and his teachers. If you change the staff in the middle of the year, I know that he will be back at square one. I am positive that it is the consistency of the staff in my son's life that has transformed him from being an unruly child to being well-behaved and making good grades."

At this point the critical tenor of the room was almost palpable, as it was certainly audible. The general fervor of the moment had gained momentum, as person after person vocalized his or her utopic discontents. All that remained was for someone, a channeler, to embody the room's accumulating fervor, ushering in an Aristotelian catharsis.

In homiletic solemnity, the acting principal proceeded to the front of the room and asked to use one of two microphones. Her narrative—epic, vulnerable, venerable, and confessional—was a public declaration of the ways that she had transformed Community Elementary School since her arrival:

"All it takes is a little creativity, because it doesn't cost a lot of money to infuse arts and beautification into the school. I have asked for volunteers to help revive some of the broken furniture and restore the room where we keep our instruments for our music program. People are helping, but we need more of you. I have over nine-hundred e-mails of grants that are coming in to help us. We have things we can do. We have parents who are willing to help. We are in the process of getting the building painted. And, although our dance program is not as big as I would like it to be at the moment, it is functioning. We have the proper dance attire, which was donated to us by Capezio. If we are phased out, we are going to leave with a fight. I am a can-do person, and I have a can-do staff. Scores are going up. They have risen about 4 percent in the last year. I don't want you to feel like you don't have choices. It is easy to turn a school around of under three hundred. What's hard is to continue to let kids fail. And it's not just about academics. It is dangerous out here. This community just buried little Frankie Johnson, who attended this school. The auditorium was filled at his memorial. I said to myself that we will NOT bury any more children because they did not have options."

She abandoned the microphone, tearful, as if she had more to say but had succumbed to the magnitude of her emotions. The entirety of her speech had traversed a backdrop of concurring nods and vocalizations. She ended to raucous applause. Beyond that point there was nothing more that could be said, especially given the fact that the hour allotted for this occasion had almost completely lapsed.

The facilitators ended the meeting with another spate of formalities and the empty, ironic directive to "let your voices be heard."

SECOND SCHOOL CLOSING MEETING

The second day of meetings was very much like the first, although this time, it was in a large conference facility rather than in an auditorium. The facilitators were positioned at the front of the room, albeit an arbitrary front, and the attendees clustered around about twenty individuated tables. This time, however, the different cast of facilitators assumed a stance that was markedly tougher than the one they had taken at the first meeting. One gentleman, who appeared to be the lead facilitator, followed the introductory remarks with a litany of statistical justifications for closing the school. His austere comportment, the rapidity with which he communicated his list, and the mathematically constituted nature of the information that he shared all lent truth value, ontological closure to his content, or rather conceits:

"The honest truth is this. . . . Let's look at the facts. Only 38 percent of the students at Community Elementary School are reading at grade level. Less than half are achieving grade level in math. We have to dig deeper. The school is having trouble making progress, as evidenced by the available data. Only three out of ten parents in the zone even elect to send their children to Community. The decision has therefore been to have the younger children attend next year, but under different administration. There will be a different approach as the new school phases in. We have confidence that the old school, as it gets smaller, will benefit students under the current administration."

A woman responded to the gentleman's comments:

"I currently look after five schools in my district. It is ironic and insulting to put a new principal in place and not give her [*motioning toward the principal of Community*] a chance to turn this school around. It is a shame and a disgrace. Before anything is closed, fix this first. I see this principal staying late and putting all her energy into this."

The lead facilitator did not answer the woman's concerns directly, but instead opted to parrot the empty refrain that persisted throughout the evening: "I know that there will be many aggrieved opinions. We want to make sure that we answer questions, since parents are here."

Another gentleman took the floor:

"In the army, we don't fire people. They retrain their leadership. Let's retrain them. We are looking at numbers and bottom lines, but let's look at other benefits to the children. What about their sense of pride? What about their self-esteem? What will happen to afterschool programs that help kids in other ways? Let's fix what we have."

A representative from the local assembly stood, identified herself, and began to question the lead facilitator: "How much of phasing out is due to budget cuts? Why not just redirect funds into what's already there rather than reinventing the wheel? It ultimately costs more to start something new anyway."

Lead representative: "Our investment has not made the desired returns. Indicators of academic success have not yielded good results."

A parent from Community Elementary School:

"Why phase out now, when parents have been advocating and asking for help for years? Parents were not heard. They have not given us what we've asked for; now they want to close the school. I stepped back because the DOE said, 'we hear your voices.' But you have not heard us because no changes have taken place, and a new charter school was phased in right under our noses."

Lead facilitator: "But the charter school is doing well."

Parent: "But why is that? You are taking from Community Elementary School."

Lead facilitator: "This is not true."

At this point a woman who was sitting at a table close to me passed to another woman a note that read: "They are still not listening to parents."

A representative from a nearby district contributed to the conversation: "Let us consider the Chancellor District Model. The Chancellor takes at-risk schools and pours resources into them. What happened as a result? The schools thrived." The man then proceeded to cite a plethora of examples of such models, which all yielded positive outcomes. He continued: "It appears, however, that you always choose this district to identify at-risk schools, change administration and create mini-entities. Numbers don't tell the whole story. There are other indicators of children's success. Each child has a gift. We need to have a vision for a school, like in the Chancellor's Model."

The lead facilitator responded: "I am a man of numbers." He then stated more statistics as evidence of the failure of Community Elementary. "These are not just numbers. These are facts." After a brief pause, he offered peremptorily, "I assume that all questions have been answered."

His final statement was met with looks and grumbles of mocking confusion, irony, and measured hostility. That final utterance was a grand slip, as it confirmed the truth of the note that was passed and of what community members had been saying all along, "They are not listening to us." That statement also confirmed the disingenuousness of the oft-repeated refrain, "Let your voices be heard. We want to hear what you have to say."

Overwhelmed with emotion, the principal of Community stood and offered another heartfelt plea:

> "I basically had to come into a mess and turn it around. And, I have been turning it around. I finally have teachers who understand the work that has to be done and know how to do it. The entire culture of the school has changed and no one from the DOE has come to see it. How can you make a decision about a school that you have not even visited?"

A gentleman took the floor and corroborated the principal's testimony: "The school is different now. When you walk into the school, you can look and feel a difference." Several others bore witness to the fact that there was an unquantifiable difference in the culture of the school and that it "feels different."

Another woman raised her hand and was acknowledged:

> "We're treating kids like pegs on a board that can be moved. This leads to instability. They are talked about as if they don't have feelings and con-

nections. Every time you change administration and switch out teachers, that's one more form of denial [to the children]."

Another woman continued this sentiment: "You don't come to or know the community and you want to make changes to it. That doesn't make sense."

A parent then addressed the facilitators more directly: "Be clear with us. We were under the impression that there is a possibility that the school might stay open. That's why we are all here. Is there a chance that it could stay open?"

The facilitators evaded her question. A woman then remarked to another who is sitting across from her, "I have been to meetings with them before and they never answer my questions."

Based on the blatant evasion, all in the room concluded that "it is a done deal," and that "the school is going to close."

A parent: "We want honesty. I see the bigger picture. There is a Starbucks on the corner. There is a Bank of America that was just built up the street. This must be a part of a larger gentrification effort. It's happening all over New York. This can't just be about the kids."

The lead facilitator responded: "We are making change. We need you to come with us."

The PTA president, tearful, stood:

"What did I take off my job for, if it's a done deal? If this was so, you should have told us at the other meetings. I lost pay. I'm not telling parents that it [the school] is closing. We are going to put up a fight."

Another parent: We have always told you what we want. And we want change. Let us be a part of the change. Don't make a decision and ask us to 'come along.'"

Another woman stood:

"I have been a teacher for fifteen years. I am not a teacher at Community Elementary, but I can see the passion of all parents and teachers who are here. As an educator, that's what you want. Teaching is not a job; it is a calling. It's a heart thing [*she touches her heart*]. Give her [*indicating the principal*] a chance to turn this situation around."

An indignant father: "We were lied to. We thought there might be a chance for change. Now we are finding out something different. Everybody knows that this must be part of a bigger change that is taking place in this neighborhood."

A district representative then remarked about the larger social function of Community: "This school has been a safe haven in the last four months.

When a child was killed, people came here to mourn and heal." She repeated the last sentence for emphasis. "If you bring another sense of loss to this community it will not go down gently."

At that point the lead facilitator, unable to stem the tide of testimonials, ended the meeting abruptly as disappointment lingered in the air.

THE BAD FAITH OF NUMBERS

In one respect, these meetings represented the collision of two discursive streams. On one hand, there was the dis-affectation of the Department of Education "advocates," who resorted to "numbers" to make their case that Community Elementary School should be phased out. In one telling statement, the lead facilitator at the second meeting established an equivalency between "numbers" and "facts." The assumption here is that the "facts" indicate some meaningful truth about the structural predicament of the school itself. The chain of non sequiturs continues, as this purported truth would invariably recommend a prescription of phasing out the school that is not working. The conflation of "numbers" and "facts," therefore, is arbitrary at best. Thus, through an unreasonable reliance on a Russellian, hyperbolic rigor, Community Elementary School achieves tropological density and ontological closure as a "damnable," "bad," "expendable" institution.

The community members understood, however, that "numbers do not tell the whole story." Theirs was an overt appeal to a rigorous intuition: a reappraisal of the numbers based on the validity of experience. Part of this story is that consistency of teachers and administrators yields positive behavioral and academic outcomes for the students. They also understood that the institution itself was more than a place where children went to be educated, but served larger social and cultural functions. It was a place of "healing," a place where positive self-esteem and personal values were nurtured, and the source of meaningful human relationships, all of which could not be readily quantified through test scores and other measures. In fact, research has confirmed what these community members knew from experience. According to some studies, the succession of teaching and administrative faculty has adverse consequences for students' academic performance, behavior, and the overall culture of the school (Meyer, Macmillan, and Northfield 2009). These community members were similarly astute to the emotional and psychological damage caused by this phase-out. One meeting attendee commented that the phase-out represented one more form of "denial" to the students and a profound sense of "loss" for a community that had already routinely dealt with child homicides and the erosion of critical community resources. Re-evoking insights from the discussion of Goluboff (2011), Reddy (2001), Coe (2008), and Ramos-Zayas (2012) in chapter 1, this sense of "loss" that would attend the closing of Community Elementary is the epiphenomenal residue of the dynamic interplay between the impending closure of the school, and the ontological closure of the symbolic system that would instantiate the closure of the school.

Another particularly charged discursive collision was the indirection and opacity of the facilitators, and the attendees' demand for openness and honesty. In the second meeting, the lead facilitator created the illusion that there was only one sensible outcome for a school that is not performing well, phasing the institution out. As has already been indicated, however, the numbers on which he based his claims were neither self-explanatory nor auto-analytical. In addition, the facilitators cast the phase in as a solution to the educational woes of Community Elementary, despite the fact that the community offered compelling testimonies about the detriments of such an intervention. And despite the fact that the school had been making cultural and academic progress with the new leadership, and had many leads for funding supplements, the DOE continued in its resolve to close the school.

The phase-out process, which was to occur over a three-year period, would likely have had significant disadvantages for those who remained during the process—a possibility that was not even considered and is completely incommensurate with the discourse of "helping" that the facilitators had crafted. According to phase-in/phase-out proposals that have been publicly released by the New York City Department of Education, as each grade phases out, teachers and guidance counselors will be "excessed" (lose their permanent positions at that school), and there will be an increase of empty seats per classroom. Because schools are funded on a per-capita basis, empty chairs mean that the school that is phasing out will receive less DOE support for classroom operations (Martinez 2010). In addition to the inevitable loss of teachers with whom students have meaningful relationships, these expenditure decreases represent a marked refusal to invest in the students and the school that is phasing out. And by extension, the DOE privileges the school that is phasing in by committing to contribute an abundance of resources.

Meanwhile, the two-year transitional period (a grade phases out each successive year) assumes an institutional structure commensurate with its tropological one: it is quite literally "expendable" and "uncared for." This is precisely the predicament in which I found The Academy. The latter was in its final two years of phasing out. The teaching staff had been downsized and had already seen several principals come and go. Such an environment was doomed to function dystopically.

Parents and well-wishers affiliated with Community Elementary saw the impending dystopic erasures as much more than assaults on their children's educational experiences and the fabric of their community, however. They were concerned that the phase-out process was part and parcel of a more encompassing apocalyptic architecture: urban gentrification.

THE POLITICS OF GENTRIFICATION: "DONE DEALS" AND THE UNDOING OF URBAN COMMUNITIES

Gentrification refers to the process through which the lower and working-class residents of a neighborhood or community are displaced by their more affluent counterparts. While often cast as an improvement upon the gentrified neighborhoods, and the fulfillment of the goal of social integration (as the beginning stages of this process involve the co-habitation of disparate socio-economic classes), the process itself presents a very different scenario. It must be understood that neighborhood "improvement" most often involves rent increases, the influx of businesses with more expensive price tags, and increased landlord harassment and evictions, all of which have the cumulative effect of driving the original inhabitants out of their communities (Newman and Wyly 2006). The weakening of critical social networks due to the attrition of the original residents and the influx of new residents results in the eventual displacement of those who do survive rent hikes (Braconi and Freeman 2004, 2002; Atkinson 2000; Marcuse 1986; Crump 2002; Merrifield 2002).

While some researchers have argued that gentrification does not even result in significant displacement (Byrne 2003, Duany 2001), there is much more compelling statistical evidence that the phenomenon does have seriously adverse consequences for urban communities nationally and internationally (Hamnet 2003, Atkinson 2000, Beauregard 1986). For instance, in Kathe Newman's and Elvin K. Wyly's analysis of displacement statistics in communities throughout New York City, the authors discovered that, in the period spanning 1991 and 2002, between 25,023 and 46,606 households were vacated due to the aggregated forces of gentrification (2006). According to the authors' data sets, these numbers amounted to 6.2 to 9.9 percent of all rental moves in New York City. Although some have even argued that these relatively low percentages are not significant in the grand scheme of things, Newman and Wyly contend that dramatic alteration to between 25,000 and 46,000 households is significant enough to raise alarm. Furthermore, the displaced are not necessarily moving to neighborhoods in which they will find more social comforts. Their new residencies tend to be in communities that are even more impoverished socially and economically (Newman and Wyly 2006).

Based on the foregoing analyses, it is within reason to argue that processes of gentrification not only attenuate the social and political fabric of urban communities, but also relegate predominantly minority populations to even more abject arrangements of poverty. Part of this unraveling involves severe compromises to local public schools—compromises which occur in two ways. Representative of one group of researchers, Ansalone and DeSena contend that gentrification is a direct catalyst for the phenomenon of resegregation that was discussed in chapter 2. In their findings, the newly arrived gentry are grossly discontent with the conditions of the local schools, and, as a result, do not enroll their children (2009). These parents send their children to more desirable schools in more affluent neighborhoods. So, while the neighborhoods are achieving an apocryphal integration (as this comingling has proven to be only a stage of an eventual mass displacement), the schools within those communities become increasingly segregated. What is more, the exodus of students from these local schools is attended by a loss of public education dollars (2009).

A second way that gentrification works to the detriment of urban communities is the phasing out and total displacement of schools. In "From Accountability to Privatization and African American Exclusion: Chicago's 'Renaissance 2010,'" Pauline Lipman and Nathan Haines present compelling archival and statistical evidence that school closing feeds neoliberal corporate agendas (2007). In other words, phase-outs and closings are handmaidens to larger corporate aims. Lipman's and Haines's work comes in the tradition of cultural geographers who examine the relationship between the spatial structuring of urban cities and neoliberal policies (Brenner and Theodore 2002; Harvey 2001; Smith 1996, 2002), and educational sociologists who specifically examine the links between urban education and gentrification (Apple 2001, 2003; Ball 1994, 2003; Dale 1989/1990; Petrovich and Wells 2005). Lipman and Haines argue that racism is central to these patterns of structuration, maintaining that racism not only plays a significant role in the accumulation of capital, but is in itself a motivating force (2007). Furthermore, race significantly affects whose voices get heard and whose are ultimately silenced. Therefore, a critical race analysis would allow us to privilege experiential knowledge—the proverbial rigorous intuition—as a legitimate source of qualitative data to understand the racial implications of school policies (Delgado Bernal 1998, Ladson-Billings 1999, Yosso et al. 2005).

A common theme in the decision to close several urban schools in Chicago's Renaissance 2010 initiative and in the decision to close Community Elementary School was that, in the days leading up to the closings, there was no invitation for the respective communities to give their input about the imminent changes. The decisions were presented as "done deals" before any input was solicited, albeit disingenuously. The cities simply made their decisions and left the existing residents, including the schoolchildren, to deal with the consequences.

CONCLUSIONS

In both Chicago and New York City, NCLB provided a justification for the cities to close schools in predominantly African American urban neighborhoods. In both cases, school board officials argued that, based on low test scores and high rates of academic failure in course work, the schools deserved to be closed and replaced by educational institutions that work. In both cases, "numbers" were reified as evidence of institutional inferiority and as an indisputable, empirical justification for why these schools should be closed. This entire scenario is an illustrative example of Cornel West's analysis of "institutional racism." For West, the deeply entrenched, institutional character of racism has the effect of proscribing the assertion of individual liberties (1982). For in making a decision to gentrify neighborhoods and close schools in the process, pedagogical, corporate, and political brokers effectively confiscate the choices of students, parents, and other community stakeholders. As one parent said in the New York case, "It's about choice. If you are only given one choice . . . that is not choice."

The closing of a school does indeed narrow the choices of the children who once attended it—they lose meaningful student-teacher and student-administrator relationships; they lose supportive networks forged by the synergy of school personnel, students, and parents; they lose options of institutions to attend; and most importantly, because of the erosion of pedagogical supports, many lose the choice of a quality education. The loss of a school also narrows the choices for the community at large, as it tends to be part of larger projects of gentrification and urban "renewal." The community loses structural and affective resources, leading to increased incidents of crime and degeneracy. The ultimate result of this gentrification/school closing macroprocess is the utter death and eradication of the community itself.

The entire scenario is indicative of the very structure of our symbolic order and its endurance from the inception of the colonial enterprise to the present day. If the system of chattel-slavery left black people with only two feasible choices—to exist in a position of inferiority or to cease to exist at all—urban poor communities and their inhabitants would seem to face but a historical updating of the same limited set of possibilities.

Chapter Nine

Recommendations

Revising Legal Discourses, Educational Policies, and Systems of Accountability

If we assume that the conditions in The Academy are representative of those in Title I schools across the country, then we could reasonably suspect that, since their institution in 2001, No Child Left Behind (NCLB) policies have, to various degrees, ruined the educational and social prospects of millions of American children. And, if there be any credence to my analysis of Community Elementary School, NCLB has also contributed to the continued demise of our nation's poor, urban communities. How could matters have concluded otherwise? Juridical discourses regarding education, their enforcement as national educational policies, and corporate real estate interests are not to be easily undone or resisted. The monograph up to this point has been a lament of sorts. Yet if we are to work toward ensuring that millions of our nation's children and thousands of communities do not continue to face the real possibility of apocalypse, where should we focus our attention?

An existential psychoanalytic anthropology would insist upon an earnest critique of discourses that I term "nomothetic," particularly the discourse of law. A brief consideration of some conspicuous omissions in the No Child Left Behind Act provides an illustrative example. Nowhere in its 670 pages does the document discuss the connection between the failure of minority students and the history of slavery and legal segregation. Furthermore, nowhere does the act include an analysis of the intimate connection between failed educational practices and the degeneracy of urban poor communities. The hypocrisy of it all is the inconsistency in the deployment of history. We revive and pay compulsory deference to historical narratives in order to confirm the sanctity of our legal order, yet ignore history when a law concerns an embarrassing contradiction within those very narratives.

We must insist at every turn, therefore, that any discourse—legal or otherwise—regarding urban education and NCLB is simultaneously a discourse upon slavery, Jim Crow, the race-based symbolic order, *Plessy*, *Brown*, the legislative neglect around the issue of desegregation plans from 1970 to 1990, the abandonment of resegregation plans in Oklahoma and Missouri beginning in 1990, the links between NCLB policies and school closings, the link between school closings and urban gentrification, and finally, the destruction of urban communities as a consequence of NCLB and the forces of urban succession.

Once we begin to acknowledge that a discussion of NCLB requires a broader field of engagement, we may also acknowledge the indispensability of knowing how administrators, teachers, and most importantly, students, are living within these policies on a daily basis. An existential psychoanalytic anthropology of educative matrices—merging the intuitional value of studying the contours of consciousness with the rigorous collection of ethnographic data—would allow us to see that each day that Crystal and Curtis attend Mrs. Beal's class, they become the victims of symbolic and affective procedures that have persisted since the colonial encounter. We would see that each day in attendance in Mrs. Beal's class means that Crystal and Curtis are also getting progressively further behind the students at Randolph. It would become apparent that The Academy's students' impending failure in school will eventually manifest itself in a failure in life, contributing to the demise of their communities. It would also become clear that, daily, Jessica and Andy experience themselves as disposable, hated, bad, inferior, and without hope. And, if we all agree that the purpose of education is to groom children to become productive, contributing members of American society, then it would be quite apparent that if Jessica, Andy, Crystal, Curtis, and Lydia are, from elementary to high school, engaged in a process of becoming hated and disposable, then these students will not fulfill this higher aim.

Another solution involves continued professional development for all stakeholders in the educational system, especially those who have direct contact with the students on a daily basis—teachers and administrators. In a study concerning how racial stereotypes inform teaching practices, Smith and Smith discovered that teachers and students would benefit tremendously from teachers' continued participation in "diversity training" (2009). And, as Sara Ahmed recommends, this diversity training would be a historically robust, psychoanalytic, phenomenological enterprise (2012). The common sense of this recommendation is virtually irrefutable. However, I would argue that the training must go far beyond diversity. If rooted in an existential psychoanalytic anthropological approach, the trainings would involve candid conversations about the tangible effects of history upon the present, and about how urban educational policies effectively vanquish poor communities of color. Stakeholders would have to be taught about the intricacies of a racist symbolic order, and how it manifests itself in educational policy. And lastly, these same stakeholders would need to confront their own racism. In short, this "training" would be more in alignment with Spillers's psychoanalysis of race (1996) and what Sartre initially proposed for an existential psychoanalytic enterprise.

With regard to policies designed to measure efficacy, "accountability" would have to be enlarged to include the daily experiences of the students. As many parents and well-wishers of Community Elementary School remarked, "numbers do not tell the whole story." For what do numbers tell us if children are subjected continuously to rituals in which their sense of self-worth, their educational and social prospects, and their very spirits are progressively destroyed? How can numbers account for the inhospitable physical conditions of the school, which research has already shown to diminish educational experiences? And finally, how can the numbers allow us to have a serious conversation about teachers' racist and classist assumptions about their students, especially when we all know that such assumptions are damaging to students at every level of their beings? Accountability measures that consist of ethnographic analyses of rituals of becoming might allow us to know exactly why certain schools are failing, which would aid us in implementing solutions that are consistent with the precise needs of a given institution. Studying these hindrances to efficacy and developing solutions might be achieved if we synthesize existential psychoanalytic anthropology and Participant Action Research (PAR), for instance. We might draw inspiration from Grace Enrique's work, which fuses phenomenological theories of being and ethnography to understand students' total experience of literacy practices (2014).

Lastly, what has been the impetus for this project in the first place and the running premise throughout this work is the notion that educational policies must take into account the voices and the experiences of the children. For in composing this book, no matter where I looked throughout the course of my research—educational scholarship, legal documents, newspaper articles, policy documents—invariably, there was a conspicuous and disturbing absence of children. Including children would constitute a departure from the data-driven focus of educational scholarship and educational policies. If the *experiences* of children are at the center of scholarship and policy, then we redefine "child" itself, restoring to this word the valence of inalienable humanity. And the more we start to see children as total human beings, the more we will start to care about how they think and feel, and who they are.

We might achieve this redefinition if we are able to achieve a more encompassing paradigm shift. To whom are schools accountable? And to whom must they answer in order to ensure their own survival? At present, schools are accountable to an entity that is made even more insidious by its generic character: the system of accountability itself. In the present era, it is the system and the system alone that must be appeased in order for stakeholders to feel any measure of security. Such an appeasement almost guarantees the divestment of our collective humanity. The mode of intersubjective exchange becomes quantitative measurement—there are no mutual disclosures of thought and feeling. Schools are reduced to letter grades, teachers to years of experience and salaries, and students to test data. The whole field of relations then becomes a grand procedure in the datafication of individual and collective beings. If American education is to repair itself, it must cease to be accountable to a faceless system of measurements. It must be accountable to the goal of achieving social equality. Above all, it must be accountable to the children.

Bibliography

Abdul-Aleem, M. (2011, December 15–21). "Black, Hispanic and special needs disproportionately suspended in New York City public schools." *The New York Amsterdam News* 33, 33.

Adams, C. R., & Singh, K. (1998). "Direct and indirect effects of school learning variables on the academic achievement of African American 10th graders." *Journal of Negro education* 67, 48–66.

Adamson, F., & Darling-Hammond, L. (2011). "Speaking of salaries: What it takes to get qualified, effective teachers in all communities." Center for American Progress. Retrieved from http://www.americanprogress.org/issues/education/report/2011/05/20/9638/speaking -of-salaries/. Accessed February 28, 2013.

Adorno, T. (1973). *Negative dialectics.* New York: Continuum International Publishing Group, Inc.

Ahmed, S. (2012). *On being included: Racism and institutional life.* Durham, NC: Duke University Press.

Ahrentzen, S., & Evans, G. W. (1984). "Distraction, privacy and classroom design." *Environment and behaviour* 16(4), 437–454.

Allen, J. (2011). *Venceremos?: The erotics of black self-making in Cuba.* Durham, NC: Duke University Press.

Amrein, A. L., & Berliner, D. C. (2002). "High-stakes testing, uncertainty, and student learning." *Education policy analysis archives* 10(18).

Ansalone, G., & DeSena, J. N. (2009, September). "Gentrification, schooling and social inequality." *Education research quarterly* 33(1), 60–74.

Apple, M. W. (2001). *Educating the "right" way: Markets, standards, God, and inequality.* New York: Routledge Falmer.

———. (2003). *The State and the politics of education.* New York: Routledge.

Atkinson, R. (2002, June). "Does gentrification help or harm urban neighborhoods? An assessment of the evidence-base in the context of the new urban agenda." Center for Neighborhood Research. Accessed online January 16, 2013.

———. (2000). "Measuring gentrification and displacement in greater London." *Urban studies* 37(1), 149–165.

Ball, S. J. (1994). *Education reform: A critical and post-structural approach.* Buckingham, UK: Open University Press.

———. (2003). *Class strategies and the education market: The middle classes and social advantage.* London: Routledge Falmer.

Bandura, A. (1977). "Self-efficacy: Toward a unifying theory of behavioral change." *Psychological review* 84, 191–215.

Barnitt, H. (2003). "Lighting for the future." *Building services journal: The magazine for the CIBSE* 25(1), 38–39.

Bartolomé, L. L. (1994). "Beyond the methods fetish: Toward a humanizing pedagogy." *Harvard educational review* 64, 7–22.

Barrier-Ferreira, J. (2008, January–February). "Producing commodities or educating children? Nurturing the personal growth of students in the face of standardized testing." *Clearinghouse: A journal of educational strategies, issues and ideas* 8(3), 138–140.

Beauregard, R. A. (1986). "The chaos and complexity of gentrification." In *Gentrification of the city*, edited by Neil Smith and Paul Williams. London: Unwin Hyman.

Bell, R. H. (1998). *Simone Weil: The way of justice as compassion*. Boulder, CO: Rowman & Littlefield.

Berliner, D. C., & Nichols, S. (2005). "The inevitable corruption of indicators and educators through highstakes testing." *Education policy studies laboratory*. Tempe: Arizona State University.

Bernard, R. (2005). *Research methods in cultural anthropology: Qualitative and quantitative approaches*. Lanham, MD: Altamira Press.

Berry, M. A. (2002). *Healthy school environment and enhanced educational performance: The case of Charles Young Elementary School*. Washington, DC: Carpet and Rug Institute.

Beveridge, T. (2010). "No Child Left Behind and fine arts classes." *Arts education policy review* 111(1), 4–7.

Bird, J. L. (2006). "Sister Stella's story." In *No Child Left Behind and the illusion of reform: Critical essays by educators*, edited by Thomas S. Poetter, Joseph C. Wegwert & Catherine Haerr, 77–90. Lanham: University Press of American, Inc.

Birt, R. E. (2004). "The bad faith of whiteness." In *What whiteness looks like: African American philosophers on the whiteness question*, edited by George Yancy, 55–64. New York: Routledge.

Bitz, M. (2004, April). "The comic book project: Forging alternative pathways to literacy." *Journal of adolescent and adult literacy*. 47(7), 574–586.

Blascovich, J., Spencer, S. J., Quinn, D., & Steele, C. M. (2001). "African Americans and high blood pressure: The role of stereotype threat." *Psychological science* 12, 225–229.

Board of Education of Oklahoma City v. Dowell, 498 U.S. 237 (1991).

Boas, F. (1940). *Race, language and culture*. Chicago: University of Chicago Press.

Boger, J. (2002, August). "Education's perfect storm? Racial resegregation, high stakes testing & school inequities: The case of North Carolina." *The resegregation of southern schools? A crucial moment in the history (and the future) of public schooling in America*. (Conference Paper).

Booher-Jennings, J. (2006, June). "Rationing education in an era of accountability." *Phi Delta Kappan* 87(10), 756–761.

Bourdieu, P. (1977). *Outline of a theory of practice*. Cambridge: Cambridge University Press.

Braconi, F., & Freeman, L. (2004, winter). "Gentrification and displacement." *Journal of the American planning association* 70(1), 39–52.

Braconi, F., & Freeman, L. (2002). "Gentrification and displacement." *The urban prospect* 8(1), 1–4.

Brenner, N., & Theodore, N. (2002). "Cities and the geographies of 'actually existing neoliberalism.'" *Antipode* 34(3), 349–379.

Brophy, J. (1983). "Research on self-fulfilling prophecy and teacher expectations." *Journal of educational psychology* 75(5), 631–661.

Brown v. Board of Education of Topeka, 347 U.S. 483 (1954).

Burke, C., & Grosvenor, I. (2003). *The school I'd like*. London: Routledge Falmer.

Byrne, J. P. (2003). "Two cheers for gentrification." *Howard law journal* 46(3), 405–432.

Comaroff, J., & Comaroff, J. (2006). Introduction to *Of revelation and revolution*. In *Anthropology in theory: Issues in epistemology*, edited by H. Moore and T. Sanders, 382–396. Maiden, MA, Oxford and Melbourne, VIC: Blackwell Publishing.

Capello, C. (2004). "Blowing the whistle on the Texas miracle: An interview with Robert Kimball." *Rethinking schools*. Retrieved from http://www.rethinkingschools.org (accessed 3 June 2010).

Carlson, C., Uppal, S., & Prosser, E. C. (2000). "Ethnic differences in processes contributing to the self-esteem of early adolescent girls." *Journal of early adolescence* 20, 44–67.

Chapman, L. (2005). "No child left behind in art?" *Art education* 58(1), 6–16.

Charlesworth, S. J. (2005). "Understanding social suffering: A phenomenological investigation of the experience of inequality." *Journal of community & applied social psychology* 15, 296–312.

Chikkatur, A. (2012). "Difference matters: Embodiment of and discourse at an urban public high school." *Education and anthropology quarterly* 43(1), 82–100.

Cho, D., & Lewis, T. (2005, May). "Education and event: Thinking radical pedagogy in the era of standardization." *SIMILE: Studies in media & information literacy education* 5(2), 1–11.

Choi, H., & Piro, J. (2009). "Expanding arts education in a digital age." *Arts education policy review* 110(3), 27–34.

Civil Rights Act (1964).

Clark, D. L., & Verstegan, D. A. (1988, October). "The diminution in federal expenditures for education during the Reagan administration." *Phi Delta Kappan* 70(2), 134–138.

Clarke, K. M. (2011, spring). "The rule of law through its economies of appearances: The making of the African warlord." *Indiana journal of global legal studies* 18(1), 7–40.

Coe, C. (2008). "The Structuring of feeling in Ghanaian transnational families." *City & society* 20(2), 222–250.

Colby, B. N. et al. (1981). "Toward a convergence of cognitive and symbolic anthropology." *American ethnologist* 8(3), 422–450.

Contrada, R. J., Ashmore, R. D., Gary, M. L., Coups Egeth, E. J. D., Sewell, A., Ewell, K., Goyal, T. M., & Chasse, V. (2000). "Ethnicity-related sources of stress and their effects on wellbeing." *Current directions in psychological science* 9, 136–139.

Contrada, R. J., Ashmore, R. D., Gary, M. L., Coups Egeth, E. J. D., Sewell, A., Ewell, K., Goyal, T. M., & Chasse, V. (2001). "Measures of ethnicity-related stress: Psychometric properties, ethnic group differences, and associations with well-being." *Journal of applied social psychology* 31, 1775–1820.

Cooper, P. (2003). "Effective white teachers of black children: Teaching within a community." *Journal of teacher education* 54(5), 413–427.

Crapanzano, V. (2004). *Imaginative horizons: An essay in literary-philosophical anthropology.* Chicago, IL: The University of Chicago Press.

Cross, B. E. (2007). "Urban school achievement gap as a metaphor to conceal U.S. education apartheid." *Theory into practice* 46(3), 247–255.

Crump, J. (2002). "Deconcentration by demolition: Public housing, poverty, and urban policy." *Environment and planning*, 581–596.

Csordas, T. J. (1990). "Embodiment as a paradigm for anthropology." *Ethos* 18, 4–47.

———. (Ed.). (1994). *From embodiment and experience: The existential ground of culture and self.* Cambridge: Cambridge University Press.

Dale, R. (1989/90). "The Thatcherite project in education: The case of the City Technology Colleges." *Critical social policy* 9, 4–19.

Davies, J. (2011). "Positive and negative models of suffering: An anthropology of our shifting cultural consciousness of emotional discontent." *Anthropology of consciousness* 22(2), 188–208.

Delgado Bernal, D. (1998). "Using a Chicana feminist epistemology in educational research." *Harvard educational review* 68, 555–582.

Desjarlais, R. (1994). "Struggling along: The possibilities for experience among the homeless mentally ill." *American anthropologist* 96(4), 886–901.

———. (1989). "Healing through images: The magical flight and healing geography of Nepali shamans." *Ethos* 17(3), 289–307.

DiPardo, A., & Schnak, P. (2004, January). "Expanding the web of meaning: Thought and emotion in an intergenerational reading and writing program." *Reading research quarterly* 39(1), 14–37.

Douglass, F. (1846). *Narrative of the life of Frederick Douglass: An American slave.* Boston, MA: Anti-Slavery Office.

Du Bois, W. E. B. (1920). *Darkwater: Voices from within the veil*. New York: Harcourt, Brace and Howe.

———. (1903). *The souls of black folk*. Chicago: A. C. McClurg & Company.

Durkheim, E. (2001). *The elementary forms of religious life*. Oxford: Oxford University Press.

Duany, A. (2001, April–May). "Three cheers for gentrification." *American enterprise magazine*, 36–39.

Earthman, G. I. (2004). "Prioritization of 31 criteria for school building adequacy." Available online at: http://www.aclu-md.org/facilities_report.pdf (accessed 4 December 2012).

Eaton, S., & Orfield, G. (1996). *Dismantling desegregation: The quiet reversal of Brown v. Board of Education*. New York: New Press.

Eisner, E. (2002). "The arts and the creation of mind." In chapter 4, *What the arts teach and how it shows*, 70–92. New Haven, CT: Yale University Press.

Eisner, E., McCrary, J., & Stullich, S. (2007). "National assessment of title I. Final report." Vol. 1. *National center for education and regional assistance*.

Enrique, G. (2014). "Embodiments of 'struggle': The melancholy, loss, and interactions with print of two 'struggling readers.'" *Anthropology & education quarterly* 45(4), 105–122.

Epstein, A. L. (1992). *In the midst of life: Affect and ideation in the world of the Tolai*. Berkeley, California: University of California Press.

Felice, L. (1981). "Black student dropout behavior: Disengagement from school rejection and racial discrimination." *The journal of Negro education* 52(4), 415–424.

Fieldnotes. (2008, August–2009, May). Personal observations collected by the author. (Unpublished).

Fieldnotes. (2009, March–May). Personal observations collected by the author. (Unpublished).

Fordham, S. (1996). *Blacked out: Dilemmas of race, identity, and success at Capital High School*. Chicago: University of Chicago Press.

Foster, G. M. (1973). "Dreams, character, and cognitive orientation in Tzintzuntzan." *Ethos* 1(1), 106–121.

Frankenburg, E., Lee, C., & Orfield, G. (2003). "A multiracial society with segregated schools: Are we losing the dream?" *Harvard civil rights project report*.

Freire, P. (1970). *Pedagogy of the oppressed*. New York: Herder and Herder.

Friedman, S. (2008). "Do declines in residential segregation mean stable neighborhood racial integration in metropolitan America? A research note." *Social science research* 37(3), 920–933.

Garoian, C. R. (2001, July). "Cyber pedagogy: performing resistance in the digital age." *Studies in arts education*, 51–71. University Park, PA: Penn State University Press.

Gates, H. L. (1988). *Signifying monkey: A theory of Afro-American literary criticism*. New York: Oxford University Press.

Geertz, C. (1973). *The interpretation of cultures: Selected essays*. New York: Basic Books.

Gill, L. K. (2012). "Situating black, situating queer: Black queer diaspora Studies and the art of embodied listening." *Transforming Anthropology* 20(1), 32–44.

Gilroy, P. (2000). *Between camps: Nations, camps and the allure of race*. London: Penguin.

Gloria, A. M., & Robinson Kurpius, S. E. (2001). "Influences on self-beliefs, social support, and comfort it the university on the academic nonpersistence decisions of American Indian undergraduates." *Cultural diversity and ethnic minority psychology* 7, 88–102.

Goluboff, S. L. (2011). "Making African American homeplaces in rural Virginia." *Ethos* 39(3), 368–394.

Gordon, L. R. (2000). *Existential Africana: Understanding Africana existential thought*. New York: Routledge.

Gordon, L. R. (1998, September). "The problem of biography in the study of the thought of black intellectuals." *Small axe: A Caribbean journal of criticism* 4, 47–63.

Gougis, R. A. (1986). "The effects of prejudice and stress on the academic performance of black Americans." In *The school achievement of minority children: New perspectives*, edited by U. Neisser, 145–158. Hillsdale, NJ: Lawrence Erlbaum Press.

Green v. County School Board of New Kent County, 391 U.S. 430 (1968).

Greene, M. (2007). "Arts and imagination: Overcoming a desperate stasis." *Contemporary issues in curriculum*, 4th ed., 32–38. Boston: Allyn and Bacon.

Grinker, R. R., & Kyungjin, C. (2013). "Border children: Interpreting autism spectrum disorder in South Korea." *Ethos* 41, 46–74.

Gunzenhauser, M. (2002, spring). "Guest editors' introduction: The shifting context of accountability in North Carolina and the implications for arts-based reform." *Educational foundations* 16(2), 3–14.

Gunzenhauser, M. G. (2006). "Normalizing the educated subject: A Foucaultian analysis of high-stakes accountability." *Educated studies: Journal of the American educational studies association* 39(3), 241–259.

Guthrie, J. (1983, spring). "The future of federal education policy." *Teachers college record* 84(3), 674.

Haerr, C. (2005). "The first day of school." In *No Child Left Behind and the illusion of reform: Critical essays by educators*, edited by Thomas S. Poetter, Joseph C. Wegwert, & Catherine Haerr, 77–90. Lanham, MD: University Press of American, Inc.

Hallam, S. (1996). *Improving school attendance.* Oxford, UK: Heinemann Educational.

Halpin, D. (2003). *Hope and education: The role of the utopian imagination.* London: Routledge.

Hamnett, C. (2003). *Unequal city: London in the global arena.* London: Routledge.

Hartman, S. V. (1997). *Scenes of subjection: Terror, slavery, and self-making in nineteenth-century America.* New York: Oxford University Press.

Harvey, D. (2001). *Spaces of capital: Towards a critical geography.* London: Routledge.

Haymes, S. (2001, August). "Pedagogy and the philosophical anthropology of slave culture." *Philosophia Africana* 4(2), 63–92.

Helms, J. (1990). *Black and white racial identity development.* Westport, CT: Greenwood Press.

Henry, P. (2000). *Caliban's reason: Introducing Afro-Caribbean philosophy.* New York: Routledge.

Heschong Mahone Group. (2003). *Windows and classrooms: a study of student performance and the indoor environment.* (Califonia Energy Commission).

Hilsdon, A. M. (2007). Introduction: Reconsidering agency—Feminist anthropologies in Asia. *Australia journal of anthropology* 18(2), 127–137.

Hollan, D. (2012). "On the varieties and particulars of cultural experience." *Ethos* 40(1), 37–53.

———. (2008). "Being there: On the imaginative aspects of understanding others and being understood." *Ethos* 36(4),475–489.

———. (2000). "Constructivist models of mind, contemporary psychoanalysis, and the development of culture theory." *American anthropologist* 102(3), 538–550.

hooks, b. (1994). *Teaching to transgress: Education as the practice of freedom.* NY: Routledge.

Hooks, D. (2008). "The 'real' of racializing embodiment." *Journal of community & applied social psychology* 18, 140–152.

Howard, S. (2006). "No child left behind: The scenes behind the act." In *No Child Left Behind and the illusion of reform: Critical essays by educators*, edited by Thomas S. Poetter, Joseph C. Wegwert & Catherine Haerr, 77–90. Lanham, MD: University Press of American, Inc.

Howe, H. (1990). "LBJ as the education president." In *The presidency and education*, edited by Kenneth Thompson, 102. Lanham, MD: University Press of America.

Hursh, D. (2005, October). "The growth of high stakes testing in the US: Accountability, markets and the decline in educational equality." *British educational research journal* 31(5), 605–622.

Hurston, Z. N. (1990). *Tell my horse: Voodoo and life in Haiti and Jamaica.* New York: Harper Collins.

Husserl, E. (1970). *Logical investigations.* New York: Humanities Press.

Irvine, J. (1990). *Black students and school failure: Policies, practices, and prescriptions.* New York: Greenwood Press.

Jackson, M. (2005). *Existential anthropology: Events, exigencies and effects.* Oxford, UK: Berghahn Books.

———. (2002, June). "Familiar and foreign bodies: a phenomenological exploration of the human-technology interface." *Journal of the royal anthropological institute* 8(2), 333–346.

———. (2012). *Lifeworlds: Essays in existential anthropology.* Chicago: University of Chicago Press.

———. (1989). *Paths to a clearing: Radical empiricism and ethnographic inquiry.* Bloomfield: University of Indiana Press.

———. (2005, spring). "Storytelling events, violence, and the appearance of the past." *Anthropological quarterly* 78(2), 355–375.

Jago, E., & Tanner, K. (1999). "Influences of the school facility on student achievement (The University of Georgia)." Available online at: http://www.coe.uga.edu/sdpl /researchabstracts/visual.html (accessed 3 November 2012).

Jameson, F. (2004). "The politics of utopia." *New left review* 25, 35–54.

Jeffrey, J. R. (1978). *Education for children of the poor: A study of the origins and implementation of the elementary and secondary education act of 1965.* Columbus, OH: Ohio University Press.

Johnson, D. (2005). High stakes : *Poverty, testing, and failure in American schools.* 2nd ed. Lanham, MD: Rowman & Littlefield Publishers, Inc.

Johnson, S. (2013, January 17–23). "City slated to close 17 schools; unions and activists angered." *The New York Amsterdam News* 10.

Jussim, L. (1989). "Teacher expectations: Self-fulfilling prophecies, perceptual biases, and accuracy." *Journal of personality and social psychology* 57(3), 469–480.

Jussim, L., & Eccles, J. (1992). "Teacher expectations II: Construction and reflection of student achievement." *Journal of personality and social psychology* 63(6), 947–961.

Karpen, D. (1993). "Full spectrum polarized lighting: an option for light therapy boxes." Paper presented at *101st Annual Convention of the American Psychological Association,* Toronto.

Kelly, H. (2010). "What Jim Crow's teachers could do: Educational capital and teachers' work in under-resourced schools." *Urban review* 42, 329–350.

Khalifa, M. (2011). "Teacher expectations and principal behavior: Responding to teacher acquiescence." *Urban review* 43, 702–727.

Killeen, J. P., Evans, G. W., & Danko, S. (2003). "The role of permanent student artwork in students' sense of ownership in an elementary school." *Environment and behavior* 35(2), 250–263.

Kirmayer, L. (2008). "Empathy and alterity in cultural psychiatry." *Ethos* 36(4), 457–474.

Klienfield, N. (2002, 31 July). "The elderly man and the sea? Test sanitizes literacy texts." *New York Times* 1.

Knez, I. (1995). "Effects of indoor lighting on mood and cognition." *Journal of environmental psychology* 15(1), 39–51.

Ladson-Billings, G. (1999). "Just what is critical race theory and what's it doing in a nice field like education?" In *Race is . . . race isn't: Critical race theory and qualitative studies in education,* edited by L. Parker, D. Deyhle, & S. Villenas, 7–30. Boulder, CO: Westview.

———. (1995). "Toward a theory of culturally relevant pedagogy." *American educational research journal* 32(3), 465–491.

Laughlin, C. D., McManus, J., & d'Aquili, E. G. (1990). *Brain, symbol and experience: Toward a neurophenomenology of consciousness.* New York: Columbia University Press.

Lee, D. T. S. et al. (2007). "Rethinking depression: An ethnographic study of the experiences of depression among Chinese." *Harvard review of psychiatry* 15(1), 1–8.

Lehrer, Keith. (2006). "Consciousness, representation, and knowledge." In *Self-representational approaches to consciousness,* edited by U. Kriegel & K. Williford, 409–419. Cambridge: MIT Press.

Lende, D. H., & Downey, G., (Eds). (2012). *The encultured brain: An introduction to neuroanthropology.* Cambridge: MIT Press, 2012.

Levine, L. W. (1978). *Black culture and black consciousness: Afro-American folk thought from slavery to freedom.* New York: Oxford University Press.

Levi-Strauss, C. (1978). *Myth and meaning.* New York: Schocken.

Levy, R. I. (1973). *Tahitians.* Chicago: University of Chicago Press.

Lewin, T., & Medina, J. (2003, 31 July). "To cut failure schools shed students." *New York Times* 1.

Lewis, T. (2010). "Paolo Freire's last laugh: Rethinking critical pedagogy's funny bone through Jacques Ranciere." *Educational philosophy and theory* 42(5–6), 635–648.

Lewis, T. (2006). "Utopia and education in critical theory." *Policy futures in education* 4(1), 6–17.

Lightfoot, S. (1978). "A child's place: A more complex view." *IRCD bulletin* 13(4), 1–9.

Lindseth, A. (2002). "Legal issues relating to school funding/desegregation." In *School desegregation in the 21st century*, edited by Rossell, Armor, & Walberg. Westport, CT: Praeger Publishers.

Lipman, P. (2004). *High-stakes education: Inequality, globalization, and urban school reform.* New York: Routledge Falmer.

Lipman, P., & Haines, N. (2007, July). "From accountability to privatization and African American exclusion: Chicago's 'renaissance 2010.'" *Educational policy* 21(3), 471–502.

Locke, R. G. (2011). "The future of a discipline: Considering the ontological/methodological future of the anthropology of consciousness, part III." *Anthropology of consciousness* 22(2), 106–135.

Lonczak, H. S., Abbott, R. D., Hawkins, J. D., Kosterman, R., & Catalano, R. F. (2002). "Effects of the Seattle Social Development Project on sexual behavior, pregnancy, birth, and sexually transmitted disease outcomes by age 21." *Archives of pediatric medicine* 156, 438–447.

Lonczak, H. S., Huang, B., Catalano, R. F., Hawkins, J. D., Hill, K. G., Abbott, R. D., & Kosterman, R. (2001). "The social predictors of adolescent alcohol misuse: A test of the social development model." *Journal of studies in alcohol* 62, 179–189.

Loux, M. (1998). *Metaphysics: A contemporary introduction.* New York: Routledge.

Lutz, B. F. (2005, December 19). "Post Brown vs. the Board of Education: The effects of the end of court-ordered desegregation." *Federal Reserve Board.*

Lutz, C., & White, G. M. (1986). "The anthropology of emotions." *Annual review of anthropology* 15, 405–436.

Mackey, N. (1993). "Discrepant engagement: Dissonance, cross-culturality and experimental writing." New York: Cambridge University Press.

Malhotra, A., & Schuler, S. (2005). "Measuring women's empowerment: Learning from cross-national research." In *Measuring empowerment: Cross-disciplinary perspectives*, edited by D. Narayan, 71–88. Washington, DC: World Bank.

Manganyi, N. C. (1981). *Looking through the keyhole: Dissenting essays on the black experience.* Johannesburg: Ravan Press.

Marcuse, P. (1986). "Abandonment, gentrification, and displacement: the linkages in New York City." In *Gentrification and the city*, edited by N. Smith and P. Williams, 153–177. London: Unwin Hyman.

Martinez, B. (2010, July 1). "More teachers to lose positions—but not pay." *Wall Street Journal.* Retrieved from http://online.wsj.com/article/SB100014240527487043346045753391426341055222-search.html?KEYWORDS=Barbara+Martinez&COLLECTION=wsjie/6month (accessed 27 February, 2013).

Marx, S. (2008). "Popular white teachers of Latina/o kids: The strengths of personal experiences and the limitations of whiteness." *Urban education* 43(1), 29–67.

Maslow, A. H., & Mintz, N. L. (1956). "Effects of esthetic surroundings: Initial effects of three esthetic conditions upon perceiving 'energy' and 'well-being' in faces." *Journal of psychology* 41, 247–254.

Maxwell, L. E. (2000). "A safe and welcoming school: What students, teachers, and parents think." *Journal of architectural and planning research* 17(4), 271–282.

Mbembe, A. (1992). "Provisional notes on the postcolony." *Africa* 62(1), 3–37.

McGee, R. (2006). *Teacher implementation of mathematics curriculum initiatives in a test-driven accountability environment: An ethnographic investigation into leadership, school culture, and teacher's attitudes, beliefs, and concerns* (Dissertation). Philadelphia, PA: Drexel University.

McGlotten, S. (2012). "Ordinary intersections: Speculations on difference, justice, and utopia in black queer life." *Transforming anthropology* 26(1), 45–66.

McGuinn, P. J. (2006). *No Child Left Behind and the transformation of federal education policy, 1965–2005.* Lawrence, Kansas: University Press of Kansas.

McKown, C., & Weinstein, R. (2008). "Teacher expectations, classroom context, and the achievement gap." *Journal of school psychology* 46, 235–261.

McNeely, C. A., Nonnemaker, J. M., & Blum, R. W. (2002). Promoting student attachment to school: Evidence from the National Longitudinal Study of Adolescent Health. *Journal of school health* 72, 138–146.

McNeil, L. (2000). *Contradictions of school reform: Educational costs of standardized testing.* New York: Routledge.

Mead, M. (2001). *Coming of age in Samoa: A psychological study of primitive youth for western civilization.* New York: Perennial Classics.

Merriam-Webster Dictionary. Accessed January 2, 2014. http://www.merriam-webster.com/dictionary
/consciousness.

Merrifield, A. (2002). "Dialectical urbanism: social struggles in the capitalist city." *Monthly review press.*

Meyer, M. J., Macmillan, R. B., Northfield, S. (2009, April–June). "Principal succession and its impact on teacher morale." *International journal of leadership in education* 12(2), 171–185.

Mimica, J. (2007). "Descended from the celestial rope: From the father to the son, and from the ego to the cosmic self." In *Explorations in psychoanalytic ethnography,* edited by Jadran Mimica, 77–105. New York: Berghahn.

Mimica, Jadran. (2007). *Explorations in Psychoanalytic Ethnography.* New York: Berghann Books, 2007.

Missouri v. Jenkins, 515 U.S. 70 (1995).

Moore, S. F., & Meyerhoff, B. G. (Eds.). (1975). *Symbol and politics in communal ideology: Cases and questions.* Ithaca, NY: Cornell University Press.

Moscinski, D. (2008, April). "Proficiency for all? A superintendent reflects on how he learned to stop complaining and love NCLB." *The education digest,* 40–42.

Nather, D. (2001, May 12). "Democrats leaving their stamp on Bush's education bill." *CQ weekly.*

National Center for Education Statistics. (2002).

National Commission on Excellence in Education. (1983*). A nation at risk.* Cambridge, MA: USA Research.

Newman, K., & Wyly, E. K. (2006, January). "The right to stay put, revisited: Gentrification and resistance to displacement in New York City." *Urban studies* 43(1), 23–57.

New York City Department of Education. (2011). "2010–2011 city-wide progress report." Retrieved from http://schools.nyc.gov/Accountability/tools/report/default.htm (accessed 10 September, 2011).

No Child Left Behind Act of 2001, Pub. L. No. 107–110, 115 stat. 1425–2094 (2002).

Noddings, N. (2007). "Teaching themes of care." *Contemporary issues in curriculum,* 4th ed., 64–70. Boston: Allyn and Bacon.

Nussbaum, M. C. (2001). *Upheavals of thought: The intelligence of emotions.* Cambridge: Cambridge University Press.

Ohnuki-Tierney, E. (1981). "Phases in human perception/conception/symbolization processes: Cognitive anthropology and symbolic classification." *American ethnologist* 8(3), 451–467.

Olaveson, T. (2001). "Collective effervescence and communitas: Processual models of ritual and society in Emile Durkheim and Victor Turner." *Dialectical anthropology* 26, 89–124.

Overgaard, S. (2008). "How to analyze immediate experience: Hintikka, Husserl, and the idea of phenomenology." *Metaphilosophy* 39, 282–304.

Parker, S. (1988). "Rituals of gender: A study of etiquette, public symbols, and cognition." *American anthropologist* 90, 372–384.

Parlmer, P. J. (2007). "The heart of a teacher." *Contemporary issues in curriculum.* 4th ed., 71–81. Boston: Allyn and Bacon.

Parmigian, G. L. (2006). "The No Child Left Behind act and containment of social change." In *No Child Left Behind and the illusion of reform: Critical essays by educators*, edited by Thomas S. Poetter, Joseph C. Wegwert, & Catherine Haerr, 77–90. Lanham, MD: University Press of American, Inc.

Petrovich, J., & Wells, A. S. (Eds.). (2005). *Bringing equity back: Research for a new era in American educational policy*. New York: Teachers College Press.

Patterson, O. (1982). *Slavery and social death*. Cambridge: Harvard University Press.

Phinney, J. S., Cantu, C. L., & Kurz, D. A. (1997). "Ethnic and American identity as predictors of self-esteem among African American, Latino, and White adolescents." *Journal of youth and adolescence* 26, 165–185.

Phinney, J. S., & Chavira, V. (1992). "Ethnic identity and self-esteem: An exploratory longitudinal study." *Journal of adolescence* 15, 271–281.

Phinney, J. S., Chavira, V., & Williamson, L. (1992). "Acculturation attitudes and self-esteem among high school and college students." *Youth and society* 23, 299–312.

Pinzur, M. (2003, 8 August). "State schools fail to meet new federal test standards: Federal, state results differ." *Miami Herald*. Miami, FL.

Plessy v. Ferguson, 163 U.S. 537 (1896).

Poetter, T. S. (2006). "The impact of NCLB on curriculum, teaching, and assessment." In *No Child Left Behind and the illusion of reform: Critical essays by educators*, edited by Thomas S. Poetter, Joseph C. Wegwert & Catherine Haerr, 1–14. Lanham, MD: University Press of American, Inc.

Poetter, T. S., Goodney, T., & Bird, J. (2004). *Critical perspectives on the curriculum of teacher education*. Lanham, MD: University Press of America.

Postert, Christian. (2012). "Emotion in exchange: Situating Hmong depressed mood in social context." *Ethos* 40(4), 453–475.

Ramos-Zayas, A. Y. (2011). "Learning affect, embodying race: Youth, blackness, and neoliberal emotions in Latino Newark." *Transforming Anthropology* 19(2), 86–104.

Ravitch, D. (2010). *The death and life of the great American school system*. New York, NY: Basic Books.

Reddy, W. M. (2001). *The navigation of feeling: A framework for the history of emotions*. Cambridge: Cambridge University Press.

Rong, L. (1996). "Effects of race and gender on teachers' perception of the social behavior of elementary students." *Urban education* 31(3), 261–290.

Rowley, S. J., Sellers, R. M., Chavous, T. M., & Smith, M. A. (1998). "The relationship between racial identity and self-esteem in African American college and high school students." *Journal of personality and social psychology* 74, 715–724.

Rubie-Davies, C. (2006). "Teacher expectations and student self-perceptions: Exploring relationships." *Psychology in the schools* 43(5), 537–552.

Russell, B. (2005). *Introduction to mathematical philosophy*. New York: Barnes and Noble, 2005.

Sanders, M. G., & Jordan, W. J. (2000). "Student-teacher relations and academic achievement in high school." In *Schooling students placed at risk: Research, policy, and practice in the education of poor and minority adolescents*, edited by M. G. Sanders, 65–82. Mahway, NJ: Lawrence Erlbaum Associates, Inc.

Sapir, D. J. (1981). "Leper, hyena, and blacksmith in Kujamaat Diola thought." *American ethnologist* 8(3), 526–543.

Sartre, J.-P. (2008). *Aftermath of war*. Translated by Chris Turner. London: Seagull Books.

———. (1950). *Baudelaire*. Translated by Martin Turnell. New York: New Directions Publishing Corporation.

———. (1993). *Being and nothingness: A phenomenological essay on ontology*. Translated by Hazel Barnes. New York: Washington Square Press.

———. (1993). *The family idiot: Gustave Flaubert: 1821–1857*. Chicago: The University of Chicago Press.

Schroll, M. (2010, March). "The future of a discipline: Considering the ontological/methodological future of the anthropology of consciousness, part 1." *The anthropology of consciousness* 21(1), 19–29.

Searle, J. (1994). *The rediscovery of the mind*. Cambridge: MIT Press.

Sellers, R. M., Rowley, S. A. J., Chavous, T. M., Shelton, J. N., & Smith, M. A. (1997). "Multidimensional inventory of Black identity: A preliminary investigation of reliability and construct validity." *Journal of personality and social psychology* 73, 805–815.

Shields, G. W. (2012). "Whitehead and analytical philosophy of mind." *Process studies* 41(2), 287–336.

Simon, G. M. (2005). "Shame, knowing, and anthropology: On Robert I. Levy and the study of emotion." *Ethos* 33(4), 493–498.

Smith, D. (2002) "The challenge of urban ethnography." In *Ethnography and schools: qualitative approaches to the study of education*, edited by Zou, Yali et al., 171–184. Oxford: Rowman & Littlefield Publishers.

Smith, N. (1996). *The new urban frontier: Gentrification and the revanchist city*. New York: Routledge.

Smith, N. (2002). "New globalism, new urbanism: Gentrification as global urban strategy." *Antipode* 34(3), 427–450.

Smith, S., & Smith, B. (2009). "Urban educator's voices: Understanding culture in the classroom." *Urban review* 41, 334–351.

Snyder, T. L. (2010, June). "Suicide, slavery and memory in North America." *The journal of American history*, 39–62.

Sommer, R. & Olsen, H. (1980) "The soft classroom." *Environment and behavior* 12(1), 3–16.

Southgate, E. (2003). *Remembering school: Mapping continuities in power, subjectivity, and emotion in stories of school life*. New York: Peter Lang Press.

Spatig-Amerikaner, A. (2012, August 22). "Unequal education: Federal loophole enables lower spending on students of color." Center for American Progress. Retrieved from http://www.americanprogress.org/issues/education/report/2012/08/22/29002/unequal-education/ (accessed 28 February, 2013).

Spillers, H. J. (1996). "'All the things you could be by now, if Sigmund Freud's wife was your mother': Psychoanalysis and race." *Boundary 2*, 23(3), 75–141.

Spring, J. (1976). *The sorting machine: National educational policy since 1945*. New York: David McKay.

Springer, M. G. (2005). "Accountability incentives: Do schools practice educational triage." *Education next* 8(1), 74–79.

St Louis, B. (2005). "Brilliant bodies, fragile minds: Race, sport and the mind/body split." In *Making race matter: Bodies, space & identity*, edited by C. Alexander & K. Knowles. London: Palgrave.

Stocking, G. (1992). "Polarity and plurality: Franz Boas as psychological anthropologist." In *New directions in psychological anthropology*, edited by Theodore Schwartz et al. Cambridge: Cambridge University Press.

———. (1968). "Franz Boas and the culture concept in historical perspective." In *Race, culture and evolution: Essays in the history of anthropology*, edited by George Stocking, 195–233. New York: Free Press.

Stuart, O. (2005). "Fear and loathing in front of a mirror." In *Making race matter: Bodies, space & identity*, edited by C. Alexander, & K. Knowles. London: Palgrave.

Studenberg, L. (2012). "Lehrer on Consciousness." *Philos studies* 161, 131–140.

Tanner, C. K. (2000). "The influence of school architecture on academic achievement." *Journal of educational administration* 38(4), 309–330.

Thompson-Shriver, M. (2009). *Education accountability in the era of no child left behind: What counts versus what matters*. (Doctoral dissertation).

Throop, C. Jason. (2005). "Hypocognition, a 'sense of the uncanny,' and the anthropology of ambiguity: Reflections on Robert I. Levy's contribution to theories of experience in anthropology." *Ethos* 33(4), 499–511

———. "On the varieties of empathic experience: Tactility, mental opacity, and pain in Yap." *Medical anthropology quarterly* 26(3), 408–430.

Throop, C. J., & Laughlin, C. D. (2009). "Husserlian meditations and anthropological reflections: Toward a cultural neurophenomenology of experience and reality." *Anthropology of consciousness* 20(2), 130–170.

Toppo, G. (2011, 5 October). "Report: Minority kids suspended." *USA Today*, 3.

Trouillot, M.-R. (2003). *Global transformation: Anthropology and the modern world.* New York: Palgrave MacMillan.

———. (1991). "Anthropology and the savage slot: The poetics and politics of otherness." In *Recapturing anthropology: Working in the present*, edited by Richard Fox, 17–44. Santa Fe, NM: School of American Research Press.

———. (1995). *Silencing the past: Power and the production of history.* Boston, MA: Beacon Press.

Turner, E. (1992). *Experiencing ritual: A new interpretation of African healing.* Philadelphia: University of Philadelphia Press.

Turner, V. (1974). *Dramas, fields, and metaphors: Symbolic action in human society.* Ithaca: Cornell University Press, 1974.

———. (1985). *On the edge of the bush: Anthropology as experience.* Tuscon: The University of Arizona Press.

———. (1969). *The ritual process: Structure and anti-structure.* Chicago: Aldine Publishing.

Tushnet, M. (1996). "'We've done enough' theory of school desegregation." *Howard law review*, 39.

Tylor, E. B. (1871). *Primitive cultures: Researches into the development of mythology, philosophy, religion, language, art, and custom.* London: John Murray.

Uhlenberg, J., & Brown, K. (2002). "Racial gap in teachers' perceptions of the achievement gap." *Education and urban society* 34(4), 493–530.

Urrieta, L. (2004, 3 September). "Assistentialism and the politics of high-stakes testing." *Urban review* 38(3), 211–226.

U.S. Department of Education, Office of Planning, Evaluation and Policy Development, Policy and Program Studies Service. (2009, August). "An exploratory analysis of adequate yearly progress, identification for improvement, and student achievement in two states and three cities, a report from the national longitudinal study of No Child Left Behind (NLS-*NCLB*)." Washington, DC.

Watanabe, M. (2007). "Displaced teacher and state priorities in a high-stakes accountability context." *Educational policy* 21(2), 311–368.

Webber, T. (1978). *Deep like the river: Education in the slave quarter community.* New York: W. W. Norton & Company.

Wei, H. (2002, April 1–5). "Teachers' responses to policy implementation: Interactions of new accountability policies and culturally relevant pedagogy in urban school reform." Paper presented at the Annual Meeting of the American educational research association in New Orleans, LA.

Weinberg, J. R. (1936). *An examination of logical positivism.* London: Kegan Paul.

Watson-Gegeo, K. A., & Gegeo, D. W. (2011). "Divergent discourses: The epistemology of healing in an American medical clinic and a Kwara'ae village." *Anthropology of consciousness* 22(2), 209–233.

Weiss, F. & Stanek, M. (2007). "Aspects of the *Naven* ritual: Conversations with an Iatmul woman of Papua New Guinea." In *Explorations in psychoanalytic ethnography*, edited by Jadran Mimica, 45–76. New York: Berghahn, 2007.

West, C. (1982). *Prophesy deliverance! An Afro-American revolutionary Christianity.* Philadelphia: Westminster Press.

Whitehead, A. N. (1929). *Process and reality.* Corrected edition (1978), edited by D. W. Sherburne & D. R. Griffin. New York: Free Press.

Whiting, G. (2006, summer). "From at risk to at promise: Developing scholar identities among black males." *The journal of secondary gifted education* 17(4), 222–229.

Wilson, B. (2001). *Listening to urban kids: School reform and the teachers they want.* Albany, NY: State University of New York Press.

Winerip, M. (2003, 12 March). "Passing grade defies laws of physics." *New York Times*, A–22 & B–7.

Winfield, L. (1986). "Teacher beliefs toward academically at-risk students in inner urban schools." *The urban review* 18(4), 253–268.

Winston, D. (2003). Interview with Patrick J. McGuinn.

Winter, G. (2004, 26 February). "Worst rates of graduation are in New York." *New York Times*.

Woodson, C. G. (1933). *The mis-education of the Negro*. Washington, DC: Associated Publishers.

Woolner, P., Hall, E., Higgins, S., McCaughy, C., & Wall, K. (2007, February). "A sound foundation? What we know about the impact of environments on learning and the implications for building schools for the future." *Oxford review of education* 33(1), 47–70.

Wright, W. (2008, September). "High-stakes math tests: How 'No Child Left Behind' leaves newcomer English language learners behind." *Language policy* 7(3), 237–266.

Yancy, G. (Ed.). (2004). *What whiteness looks like: African American philosophers on the whiteness question*. New York: Routledge.

Yosso, T. J., Parker, L., Solórzano, D. G., & Lynn, M. (2005). "From Jim Crow to affirmative action and back again: A critical race discussion of racialized rationales and access to higher education." *Review of research in education* 28, 1–26.

Youdell, D. (2004, July). "Engineering school markets, subjectivating students: the bureaucratic, institutional and classroom dimensions of educational triage." *Journal of educational policy* 19(N), 407–431.

Youdell, D. & Gillborn, D. (2000). "Rationing education: Policy, practice, reform and equity." Buckingham, UK: Open University Press.

Zahavi, D. (2007). "Subjectivity and the first-person perspective." *The southern journal of philosophy* 45, 66–84.

Zirkel, S. (2005, 11 June). "Ongoing issues of racial and ethnic stigma in education 50 years after Brown v. Board." *Urban review* 37(2), 107–126.

Index

About the Author

Dr. Darian Marcel Parker is a psychological anthropologist who does work in existentialism, phenomenology, educational philosophy, Africana existentialism, literary criticism, and neuroanthropology, among other topics. He earned his PhD, M. Phil, and MA from Yale University's departments of anthropology and African American studies, and BAs in English literature and anthropology from UCLA. He is the founder and CEO of Parker Academics (www.parkeracademics.com), an innovative academic services company that provides a neuro-existential approach to test prep and academic subjects tutoring.

CPSIA information can be obtained at www.ICGtesting.com
Printed in the USA
BVOW08*0959051215

428365BV00002B/3/P